**SEMINAR STUDIES IN HISTORY**

General Editor: Roger Lockyer

# Charles I
# 1625–1640

## Brian Quintrell

D1167101

**LONGMAN**

**London and New York**

Addison Wesley Longman Limited
*Edinburgh Gate, Harlow,*
*Essex CM20 2JE, England*
*and Associated Companies throughout the world.*

Published in the United States of America
by Addison Wesley Longman Inc., New York

First published 1993
Third impression (with corrections) 1996

*Set in 10/11 point Baskerville (Linotron)*
*Produced through Longman Malaysia, TCP*

ISBN 0 582 00354 7

**British Library Cataloguing in Publication Data**
Quintrell, B. W.
   Charles I, 1625–40. – (Seminar Studies in History Series)
   I. Title II. Series
   941.06092

     ISBN 0-582-00354-7

**Library of Congress Cataloging-in-Publication Data**
Quintrell, Brian.
   Charles I, 1625–1640 / Brian Quintrell.
     p.    cm. — (Seminar studies in history)
   Includes bibliographical references and index.
   ISBN 0-582-00354-7 : £4.75
   1. Charles I, King of England, 1600–1649. 2. Great Britain —
Politics and government — 1625–1649. I. Title. II. Series.
DA395.Q56   1991
941.06′2–dc20
                                         92-28086
                                            CIP

# Contents

*Contents*

# Seminar Studies in History

## Introduction to the series

Under the editorship of a reputable historian, Seminar Studies in History covers major themes in British and European history. The authors are acknowledged experts in their field and the volumes are works of scholarship in their own right as well as providing a survey of current historical interpretations. They are constantly updated, to take account of the latest research.

Each title has a brief introduction or background to the subject, a substantial section of analysis, followed by an assessment, a documents section and a bibliography as a guide to further study. The documents enable the reader to see how historical judgements are reached and also to question and challenge them.

The material is carefully selected to give the advanced student sufficient confidence to handle different aspects of the theme as well as being enjoyable and interesting to read. In short, Seminar Studies offer clearly written, authoritative and stimulating introductions to important topics, bridging the gap between the general textbook and the specialized monograph.

*Seminar Studies in History* were the creation of Patrick Richardson, a gifted and original teacher who died tragically in an accident in 1979. The continuing vitality of the series is a tribute to his vision.

*Roger Lockyer*

## The General Editor

Roger Lockyer, Emeritus Reader in History at the University of London, is the author of a number of books on Tudor and Stuart history including *Buckingham,* a political biography of George Villiers, first Duke of Buckingham, 1592–1628, and *The Early Stuarts: A Political History of England 1603–1642.* He has also written two widely used general surveys – *Tudor and Stuart Britain* and *Habsburg and Bourbon Europe.*

# Part One: The Background

## 1 The Jacobean Legacy

'We live,' said William Laud, Bishop of St Davids, in his sermon at the opening of Charles's first Parliament in June 1625, 'to see a miracle, change without alteration: another king, but the same life-expression of all the royal and religious virtues of his father; and no sinews...shrinking in the State' (**31**, vol. 1, p. 98). Charles's succession was the first since 1509 to be entirely straightforward; but change was in the air, and Laud, although long in the royal service, did not in his own person entirely bear out his confident words. His new-found prominence at Court owed little to James and much to the support of the Duke of Buckingham and the new King. To the Court at large, too, change was more immediately evident than continuity. Charles remained faithful to his father's favourite, Buckingham, who had become his constant political ally [**doc. 3**]; but he had lost little time in introducing a new regimen, restoring an Elizabethan concern for proper forms, decorum and order in place of his father's characteristically relaxed ways. He intended, as he later put it, 'to establish government and order... [there] which from thence may spread with more honour thorough all parts of our kingdoms' (**188**, p. 171). But James had never seen his Court as an exemplar in this way; and it would be wrong to conclude that Jacobean England had been grievously ill-regulated or that a loosely ordered Court was necessarily an ineffectual one. James's Court was merely following the more relaxed style familiar in France and Scotland.

This qualification deserves emphasis, as prevailing fashions in English historiography, whether Whig or Marxist, have seldom been kind to James. So much is this so that the scathing comments of Sir Anthony Weldon, a minor courtier upset by his dismissal for insulting the Scots, for many years provided the popular image of James I and his Court, after being given new currency in the nineteenth century. Weldon's more balanced final assessment of James has had less prominence (**2**). Historians of Scotland have generally shown an acuter awareness of his qualities as James VI, and recently one of them, Jenny Wormald, has asked whether

James VI and I should be regarded as 'two kings or one?' (**219**). It is a question both pertinent and timely, as James has in recent years begun to escape from the hapless supporting role in impending disaster to which traditional English historiography assigned him. The hoary Whiggish assumption of a 'high road to civil war', along the early stretches of which James was commonly held to have stumbled, has finally been undermined by further search for the origins, and the mechanics, of the breakdown of Stuart government under Charles (**88**).

Instead, a number of historians, known collectively but not entirely accurately as 'revisionists' (for they form no school and do not always accept the label), have, in pursuing shorter-term explanations of the Civil War's origins, stressed the low-key nature of much of early modern government. They have established, for example, that relations between Crown and Parliament were by no means always combative, and that much was done, even in the Commons, in a cordial and cooperative way. Enjoyment of royal patronage, and the need to retain royal favour, almost invariably exercised a constraining influence. There was no sharp division between 'Court' and 'country' (**82**, Introduction). The Commons themselves were much concerned with local issues, and even in the tensest session it was not uncommon for the bulk of the legislation to be of a private or local kind. Indeed, it has been argued that this local concern inhibited MPs, discouraging close interest in national and international affairs, and making them so reluctant to commit their constituents to taxation for such purposes that the Commons were in danger of proving an irrelevance to the demands of war during the 1620s. Views were not polarised during the parliamentary tussles of these years, and there was no necessary prelude to the breakdown of government in 1640 (**178**). Other historians, who might be called 'post-revisionists', fully accept the Commons' concern with local issues, but maintain that MPs were perfectly capable of combining it with an active interest in the wider world; and that, while relations between the Crown and Parliament were frequently harmonious and cooperative, the Commons never lost sight of the need to protect parliamentary privilege and the property rights of the subject, as they showed in 1604 and 1610 (**82**). If taxation was not always readily forthcoming in the 1620s, it was primarily because the political will was lacking. And if that was the case, serious – and perhaps momentous – parliamentary conflict could not be far away (**113**, **204**).

From such historiographical debates, James emerges moderately well. His relations with his Parliaments were always patchy, and his efforts to increase his revenues were always likely to arouse fears about his subjects' property; but particularly in his early years, his misunderstandings may often be traced to lack of accurate counsel from his ministers, who had their own axes to grind, and to the unhappy influence of his Bedchamber officers (**77**). As a consequence, he failed to secure either the full union he wanted between his kingdoms or the sorely needed reforms of royal finances. More constructively, his Scottish upbringing had given him a life-long interest in the making and enforcement of legislation, as he insisted both to Prince Henry in his *Basilikon Doron* and to his early Parliaments, and he quickly appreciated the problems for central and local administrators of the tangled mass of Tudor statutes which urgently needed to be digested and codified (**26**). His fondness for royal proclamations, which dealt with specific pressing problems, stemmed from this concern rather than, as some MPs feared, from a readiness to use his prerogative to make law outside parliamentary statute (**29**).

James's financial position was, however, never secure. He hoped to overcome the weakness of his Elizabethan inheritance by taking advantage of the Exchequer's apparently hopeful verdict in the case of the malcontent Turkey merchant John Bate in 1606 to create a solid annual source of ordinary revenue through an extension of the customs, beyond the limits set by statutory regulation of tonnage and poundage (**28, 76**). But this took time, and by 1618, when the Thirty Years' War broke out, he was scarcely better equipped to face heavy demands for extraordinary, wartime expenditure than Elizabeth I had ever been. Such demands were, however, almost inevitable after his son-in-law, the Elector Palatine Frederick V, had been forcibly removed by vengeful Habsburg forces both from the throne of neighbouring Bohemia, which he had recently accepted against James's advice, and from his hereditary Palatinate. The exile of James's firmly Calvinist daughter Elizabeth and her children at the Hague, while Frederick struggled to recover his fortunes, daily emphasised the blow to Stuart honour. If diplomacy failed, funding for war might well be needed (**116, 164**).

This situation brought into sharper focus the delicate and ill-defined relationship between the granting of supply by the Commons and the remedying by the Crown of the grievances they put before it (**69** and, e.g., **doc. 11**). In 1621 James got the supply he asked for early, and without discussion of grievances, but even

3

though the circumstances warranted speed, the Commons first devoted a week to considering whether a recent proclamation, forbidding anti-Spanish comment while the King was engaged in the protracted negotiations for a Spanish match for Charles, infringed their freedom of debate (**124**). The second session, later that year, was to end abruptly without further supply, after a more celebrated difference of opinion over the extent to which the Commons were entitled to proffer advice on foreign policy. They also felt let down by James's failure to respond to their rapid grant of supply in the first session by allowing them time for a thorough consideration of grievances in the second. Many completed bills thereby failed to get the royal assent. But in essence, James's view of foreign policy prevailed. Diplomacy with Spain was preferable to the cost and hazards of military confrontation with occupying Habsburg forces, for the English had no regular army of their own. Any Protestant crusade would have to wait (**145**).

In 1624, after Charles's dramatic but fruitless dash with Buckingham to Madrid had at least exposed the hollowness of Spanish interest in bringing about the release even of the Lower Palatinate, on the Rhine, which had fallen to Spinola's troops in 1620, James himself first publicly proposed to Parliament that supply should be appropriated to specific defensive purposes, which might precede a war, and his ministers made accountable to the Commons for the way it was spent; but the Commons had toyed with this arrangement in 1621, and may well have suggested it to James in 1624 (**28**). For the possibility of war remained the central issue; and although no fewer than thirty-five public acts and thirty-eight private ones were passed in 1624, which might suggest a Parliament with its mind on domestic matters, most had been prepared for the royal assent in 1621, and scarcely needed further discussion (**140**, cf. **178**). There were important tactical and procedural lessons here for Charles, if he could see them. As Tom Cogswell has shown, the Commons were less supine and irrelevant in the face of war than revisionists have sometimes supposed (**69, 70**, also **120**). While there was no crude bargaining for redress of grievances before supply, of the kind Whig historians once assumed, James's experiences nevertheless demonstrated that there existed an intangible but powerful relationship between the two which it ill behove a king to ignore.

However important its role, Parliament was, even during the 1620s when five general elections were held, comparatively seldom in session. It had little claim to be regarded as part of the King's regular administration. Much more central to his affairs, as revisionist historins have pointed out, were the Court and the Privy Council. James's lengthy experience of direct participation in government in Scotland through his Chamber there led him in 1603 to amplify the role of the Bedchamber within the Household and to try to make it the centrepiece of his rule over his two kingdoms (**77**). It was an imaginative idea, but it meant grafting Scottish practice onto the more formal structure favoured by Elizabeth I, and was only partially successful. Early problems over the continuing preponderance of Scots among its members and restricted access to the King for English ministers gave way in time to problems over the influence of Buckingham, who, with Prince Charles, used the Bedchamber as a base from which to press on James their distinctive views on foreign policy. Buckingham kept his critics from the King so effectively that by late 1624 there was visible unrest within the Privy Council at the selective nature of the advice taken. One of its senior members, the hispanophile Earl of Arundel, protested to Charles in January 1625 at the way he and others were being excluded from royal counsels, complaining that while they could see what was happening they had no knowledge of how or why decisions had been arrived at (**145**). Buckingham thus began to seem to courtiers like Arundel and the Lord Chamberlain, the Earl of Pembroke, to have too large a part not just in dispensing the King's patronage but also in deciding the nature of his policy (**147**). There was ground here on which parliamentary suspicions might grow.

James was never as familiar a figure at administrative meetings of his English Privy Council as he had been at its Scottish counterpart; but he attended rather more often than Elizabeth had ever done, and took a particular interest in matters of trade and commerce – now a source of much of his revenue – and in both 1616 and 1620 presided on half a dozen occasions (**1**). With Sir Francis Bacon, he seems to have believed that he had a duty to lend majesty to its proceedings, but not so often that his councillors felt inhibited and ceased to debate freely (**43**). As Bacon's own papers show, the Council and the common law judges who rode the assize circuits twice each year were capable of setting exacting standards of performance under pressure from the King, who expected straight answers about the country's problems and encouraged his officials to do the same. As early as 1607 he was boasting that he had dealt personally with his common law judges more often than his predecessors had done; and even though he clashed with them over their attitude to the prerogative (equity) and ecclesiastical courts, he also encouraged them to take a wider responsibility for the condition of England (**29, 43**). Even in the early 1620s, when he was once supposed to be losing his grip, James with his Council launched into an extensive series of enquiries into persistent financial and commercial problems by commissions which included not only councillors but also MPs and City merchants (**72, 139**).

In his handling of the Church of England, James showed he had learned in Scotland the benefits of argument and discussion in reaching acceptable decisions; and, scholar that he also was, he did not shy from entertaining views other than his own. His Church of England was a broad one and, until the Thirty Years' War brought its tensions, contained fairly comfortably within it a wide range of Protestant opinion either side of his own deliberately less well-defined one. His renewed attempts at a Spanish marriage for Charles, however, once more stirred anti-popish elements in the Church, and caused James to shift his favours at Court away from his rigidly Calvinist primate, George Abbot, towards other clergy, anti-Calvinist (or, more loosely, Arminian), who were prepared to accept such a match, a process helped by the deaths of the two most influential courtly Calvinists, James Montagu, Bishop of Winchester (1618) and John King, Bishop of London (1621) (**91, 92**). He inclined more noticeably towards an ambitious group of anti-Calvinist clergy, gathered nearby around Bishop Neile at Durham House. He also advanced another old enemy of Abbot, John Williams, to the see of Lincoln and then to the office of Lord Keeper (**213**).

In this changing context, Richard Montagu, royal chaplain, Canon of Windsor and on the fringe of the Durham House circle, began to make a name for himself. In 1624, he published *A New Gagg for an Old Goose*, which was calculated to appeal to James in his present circumstances, while undermining the Calvinist position within the Church. He was aware of James's pride in his role as a Christian peacemaker and in his belief in the apostolic catholicity of the Church of England, but argued that James's criticism of Rome for failing to put its doctrinal house in order would sound better if he had done the same to the Church of England. In Montagu's eyes, there were very few major differences in doctrine between the two churches; but the most obtrusive was one central to orthodox Calvinist belief: the relationship between predestination*, grace and free will, the Calvinist interpretations of which he regarded as both puritan and schismatic. Within a year, in the face of Abbot-inspired rumblings at Court and in Parliament, Montagu published the shrewdly entitled *Appello Caesarem* (1625), a work James himself licensed for the press. In this Montagu pushed still further the case for regarding Calvinism as an open door to subversion (**91, 92, 213**, cf. **217**).

As James died shortly afterwards, it is difficult to assess how truly convinced he was by Montagu, or how far he was simply making tactical use of his work as a means of distancing himself from the strident anti-Spanish sentiments of Charles and Buckingham. He had recently been reminded of the enduring strength of Calvinist feeling within the Church. Anxious to prevent the lower clergy from inflaming passions against the Spanish match, he had in August 1622 issued a series of cautionary Directions to preachers (**28**). Yet even before the prospects of the marriage finally faded a year later, Calvinist clergy were openly flouting his instructions. In this there was, perhaps, a lesson for Prince Charles. Certainly, at James's death his Church was still, in its policy-making and its administration, firmly in Calvinist hands (**213**).

James's death in March 1625 was comparatively unexpected. Few mourned him, although there was much concern for security reasons at the manner of his dying. But as he himself had remarked years before in *Basilikon Doron*, 'although a King be never so precise in the discharging of his office, the people who seeth but the outward part, will ever judge of the substance by the circumstances' (**26**, p. 43). Dying as he did at a politically awkward moment, James has, it seems, been misjudged almost ever since.

# 2 Charles's Apprenticeship

Unlike his father, Charles was not born to rule. His childhood was privileged, but scarcely favoured. Although he escaped the debilitating attacks of porphyria which dogged James, and which probably accounted for his elder brother Henry's early death in November 1612, he was so sickly a child that his parents left him behind in Scotland in 1603 and subsequently had difficulty placing him, as English courtly households were fearful that he would die on their hands (**149**). At the age of four he was unable to walk 'nor scant stand alone' according to Sir Robert Carey, to whose wife Charles's welfare was eventually entrusted (**101**, p. 11). Born at Dunfermline in November 1600, Charles was several years younger than Henry (born in February 1594) and Elizabeth (born in August 1596), and spent much of his childhood separated both from them and from his parents. He was never to have much personal contact with his brother and sister; for by 1612, as Charles grew stronger, James was already exercised about the marriages of his elder children. For diplomatic reasons, he hoped to marry Henry into a Catholic royal family, and Elizabeth into a Protestant one. Henry had Catholic friends, but his Calvinism was strong and he had other ideas (**188**). He worked hard, using his developing range of continental contacts, to further the marriage of his sister to the most important of the Calvinist princes, Frederick of the Palatinate. He died on the eve of the marriage, before putting his father to the test over his own reluctance to take a Catholic wife (**198**). Within a few months, during the winter of 1612–13 Charles, in the absence of both his parents, led the mourners at Henry's funeral, and for the last time, as it was to turn out, bade farewell in person to Elizabeth and Frederick, after lingering with them at Canterbury on their way to the coast. The contacts which he had begun to make with his family thus rudely shaken, he resumed his solitary state, but this time as heir to the thrones not only of England and Ireland, but of his native Scotland too. He had twelve years in which to accustom himself to an unprecedented inheritance.

Although Charles now began to see more of his Catholic mother,

Anne of Denmark, sister of Christian IV, a cultivated woman with a life and court of her own, he found it difficult to get on terms with his father. The favourites, Somerset and then Buckingham, were in the way. James did not entirely neglect him, however, and there was talk of a possible French marriage during 1613, before the Spanish ambassador Sarmiento (later Count of Gondomar) for the first of many times raised the prospect of a union between Charles and the Infanta Donna Maria, who was of similar age. Whatever happened, James was determined on a Catholic wife for him. He took Charles to the opening of the 1614 Parliament, and there in the early formalities the Prince heard his father explain his reasons for the Palatine match. But gratification at England's new continental foothold was mingled with widespread expressions of regret at what had been taken away. The outpouring of elegies after Henry's death had already begun to encourage the creation of a potent myth, that England had lost the Protestant champion it desperately needed (**124**). Certainly, Henry's vigorously Protestant approach to foreign policy had provided a counterbalance to his father's carefully weighted diplomacy. James may even have intended that it should, before becoming concerned at the extent of Henry's influence (**188**). Possibly as a consequence, he gave Charles, to whom it must now fall to sustain or disappoint such hopes, less scope for independent activity. He may also have noticed how similar the two brothers were, despite the differences in their upbringing. Both ordered their affairs with strict regularity. They shared the same cold personality, stiff and formal manner, and self-centred concern with cultural patronage which made them difficult to know well. Henry's popularity had owed more to his militant Protestantism than to his personality. Whatever James's reason, Charles in the years ahead showed himself less assertive than Henry had been, slow to express his opinion, and noticeably anxious not to cross his father.

When at last James managed in 1617 to visit Scotland – which he had originally intended to do every few years – he took Buckingham with him; but despite Charles's express wish to visit his native land and to learn its customs, he was allowed to accompany the royal party no further than Huntingdon on the journey north. Charles became instead a member of the small council left to govern England; but given his insensitivity to, and disregard of, Scottish ways in 1625, an opportunity arguably was lost. Better still, James might have given him the chance of an extended stay in Scotland, since not all those who did accompany

James on his brief visit managed – or had the inclination – to develop an appreciation of the distinctive preferences of another country. James's celebrated criticism of Laud, as reported by John Hacket, an unfriendly source, that 'he hath a restless spirit and cannot see when matters are well, but loves to toss and change and to bring things to a pitch of reformation floating in his own brain, which may endanger the steadfastness of that which is in a good pass', was made after he had clashed with his chaplain in Scotland over the moderate nature of the articles of Perth (**18**, part 1, p. 64).

Instead, and perhaps primarily for financial reasons, Charles was encouraged to succeed Henry as Duke of Cornwall, and in June 1615 was formally vested with the office by his father. Effectively organised, the Duchy was capable of supporting a prince's court; but it had been neglected by the Tudors. Just before his death Henry had begun both to recover lands improperly alienated by Elizabeth I and to revise the terms of his tenants' leases, seemingly intent on tying them more closely to himself as duke. According to his former treasurer, Sir Charles Cornwallis, Henry had seen the need to 'shew his authority [and]... having...avoided and annihilated all their former rights and leases he brought them unto a general submission to compound, take and hold new of him' (**33**, vol. 2, p. 375), and, but for his death, would have granted the new leases himself. His approach clearly appealed to Charles. By 1621, however, sufficient disquiet had been generated within the Duchy for the Prince to seek an act of Parliament – which was among those which belatedly received the royal assent in 1624 – to reassure tenants for lives that the new leases would have legal effect beyond the span of his own life, so that they might 'be incouraged to bestow charges in the building and maintaining of their houses and good manuring of the...land'. A new act was among the first passed by Parliament in 1625 to clarify further the position after Charles had, unusually, retained the Duchy Council on becoming King. The Cornish MP Sir John Eliot noted that it 'had aspect but to the profit of the King, though with some shadow and pretence of advantage to the tenants'; but while providing welcome administrative continuity, it also tied those tenants immediately to their duke (**36**, p. 526, *Negotium Posterorum*).

A series of events in 1619 and 1620 helped Charles to emerge from his shell. His mother died in March 1619, and with his father so ill at Newmarket that for eight days his life was in danger, Charles was left to attend Anne's deathbed and manage her funeral. He was also formally briefed on what would happen if James died. At this juncture, he seems to have become much closer to Buckingham, perhaps because the favourite had for the first time become aware of the pull of the reversionary interest (**145**, p. 56). In the autumn of the following year, Frederick and Elizabeth were expelled from Bohemia; and Charles, when he heard the news, spent two days shut in his room. But soon the Venetian ambassador, who had also begun to pay him special heed, was able to report that he had spoken strongly at the Council table, pressing the case for the German Protestant Union, as he already had on his father, encouraging like-minded Councillors and dismaying others (**6**, 11 October 1620). His performance in the Lords in the 1621 Parliament was, however, naive; and neither he nor James wanted Frederick and Elizabeth to seek refuge in England, apparently fearful that they would lend new strength to memories of Henry, and possibly cause factional complications which might affect the succession.

As a further indication of his growing assurance, however, Charles, with the support of Buckingham, took the initiative in the ever-elastic marriage negotiations with Spain which James had for many years put in the hands of John Digby, recently rewarded with the earldom of Bristol. Together, they persuaded James to agree to their going, incognito, to Madrid to conclude the marriage – now in the interest of the Palatinate cause – and bring back the infanta, Donna Maria. Gondomar had suggested in 1618 that Charles needed to visit Madrid to hurry proceedings along, and Gustavus Adolphus of Sweden had recently undertaken an uncannily similar enterprise in north Germany; but if the idea was not a new one, the grounds on which the expedition was undertaken were still difficult for many to understand. If the marriage was as close to completion as the Court claimed, why did Charles not go in the style appropriate to his rank and purpose? If it was not, why was he going at all? It is possible to find explanations in terms of Charles's physical frustrations, but not in those of political judgement. The mission was little short of a fiasco, and turned Charles's concern for the Palatinate cause also into a matter of avenging his personal honour [**doc. 1**]. During its course, he and Buckingham had made potentially embarrassing religious concessions, as the ambassador, Bristol, well knew. Remarkable celebrations greeted Charles's homecoming in October 1623, when in spite of the rain the City of London 'seemed to bee on fire', so many were the welcoming bonfires, and he enjoyed his one moment of genuine popularity. But they were fuelled by relief, not pride in achievement (**13**, p. 162; **75**).

By the time Charles and Buckingham set out for Spain they had begun to form an active political partnership. While Buckingham kept close to the King, who was often in the country, and controlled access to him, Charles began to assert himself at Whitehall in both 'high policy' and administrative meetings of the Privy Council (**145**). He had been introduced informally to the Council as early as July 1616, but until his formal admission on 26 March 1622, had only attended irregularly in the presence of James and Buckingham. Since James still made policy, the crucial discussions were held in the Bedchamber rather than at the Council table: the Council, for example, only knew of the journey to Madrid after it had begun. The pair were, as Arundel later suggested, thus open to the charge that they foisted policy onto the King's counsellors, and made it difficult for them to discuss matters with James in person. They continued in much the same way after their return, aided by James's illness; as Sir Edward Zouch noted that November, Charles was 'entering into command of affairs...and all men address themselves unto him' (**5**, 5 November 1623). In Parliament the following February, he and Buckingham offered a vigorous, if not wholly convincing, lead in foreign policy in contrast to James, whose depth of experience persuaded him to move so circumspectly that there was some doubt about what means he really favoured for seeking the recovery of the Palatinate (**70**), [**doc. 1**].

The Scots, however, were the first to feel the full force of Charles's methods and to have more lasting grounds for questioning his political judgement (**84**, **150**). While still a minor, he had been given charge of the lands of the principality in Scotland; and by January 1625 was seriously, but with some secrecy, discussing the processes by which he might revoke all grants of its lands, made during that minority, to the detriment of his interest [**doc. 2**]. Within weeks of becoming King, however, he had an altogether more sweeping plan in mind. Even while the final arrangements for his marriage to Henrietta Maria were being concluded, and elections held for his first English Parliament, he was preparing to apply the well-established process of revocation (or annexation to the Crown) of all existing grants and leases of Crown and Church property to the whole Scottish kingdom. He ignored, or pretended ignorance of, the customary provision that it concerned only monarchs who had succeeded as minors (possibly because most of them did so in Scotland), just as he did a further provision that it applied only to the most recent minority: instead, he reached back at least until 1540, and in most respects back almost two centuries to the reign of James II of Scotland. He also substantially broadened the scope of the revocation to include as much as he could of the revenues and properties which the pre-Reformation Church had once possessed. He did, however, observe the convenient provision that any revocation had to be completed between the new monarch's majority and his twenty-fifth birthday, which for Charles was rapidly approaching. An initial order for the principality was ready by 14 July, and a more sweeping one for the whole kingdom passed the Scottish Privy Seal on 12 October. His Scottish Privy Council knew little about it, having been allowed only a formal reading at some later date, which they found difficult to take in. Copies of the text were only made available after a request by an indignant and alarmed delegation of Scottish Councillors to Whitehall for an uncomfortable series of meetings with the King in the early months of 1626. Buckingham, who also took part, they found much more conciliatory [**doc. 8**].

Yet this 'authoritarian sophistry', as Allan Macinnes has called it, had aims which were by no means entirely disreputable (**150**, p. 54). Charles intended to regrant the lands in such a way that ministers, colleges, schools and hospitals were better maintained in future; the feudal superiorities of the lords of erection – that aristocracy of service granted Church lands as reward for public office, often by James VI – were curbed, to the benefit of their social inferiors; and the patrimony of the Crown was defined and recovered. What a programme of such range and sensitivity needed was that it should be done as openly and as reassuringly as possible, with maximum consultation. Charles's surreptitious and tendentious behaviour provoked alarm and a storm of criticism, which, despite subsequent explanations, took several years to subside. It all seemed much more threatening than it turned out to be: much of the land returned on new terms to its former holders; the Crown's revenues did not benefit excessively; and the Church became much more financially secure. Parts of the programme were to endure into the present century.

But here, as on a smaller scale also in the Duchy of Cornwall, Charles's determination to have grantees and leaseholders directly dependent on him aroused worries about the long-term legal status of his actions, when he would no longer be alive. Throughout, he seems to have assumed that what he wanted done should be done, regardless of convention and the feelings of those affected [**doc. 8** ii]. The revocation, with other changes then made to Scottish government, scarcely constituted a politic beginning. By 1625 he had shown himself to be a prince who elevated authority and order above all else. He had also given an indication of his concern for loyalty, and his lack of assurance that he could, simply by virtue of kingship, command it. The veiled but gratuitous threat at the end of his letter to the burgh council of Edinburgh that same year about their forthcoming elections seems, in its limited context, to confirm that impression [**doc. 5**].

Because, as the Tuscan ambassador put it in 1625, 'it is obvious that His Majesty will insist on being obeyed', Charles was seldom disposed to give explanations for his actions, unless he had some political purpose for doing so (**21**, p. 7). His apparent discomfort in public speaking may well have had as much to do with his reluctance to reveal himself, or to engage with counter-arguments, as with physical disability. His household servants, like Sir Roger Palmer, had already grown accustomed to interpreting his gestures as a guide to his meaning [**doc. 6**].

That the origins of Charles's religious convictions remain hidden is not surprising; and it is not entirely clear when he first revealed that he did not embrace the Calvinist enthusiasms of his brother and sister. Two of the chaplains with him in Madrid were from that ambitious anti-Calvinist group of clergy gathered around Bishop Neile at Durham House, with ready access to the Court; yet their leaders still found it necessary on Charles's return to consult, behind locked doors, with one of them, Matthew Wren, 'how the Prince's heart stands to the Church of England', in order to receive the assurances they hoped for (**213**, pp. 113–14; **211**). Months later, Richard Montagu, the fate of whose controversial works might yet provide a more public guide to Charles's preferences, still knew so little of the new King that he was initially dismayed when he heard of the death of James (**12**). In no sense was Charles an easy man to get to know.

# Part Two: Analysis – The War Years, 1625–1629

## 3 Parliament and War Funding, 1625

Charles opened his first Parliament on 18 June 1625 with a speech so brief that a subsequent purchaser of its printed text could not believe it was complete (**36**, pp. 28–30; **175**, p. 86). It contained one central point, several times reiterated: that the previous Parliament, which he regarded as father to the new one, had advised James to break the recent treaties (or negotiations) with Spain, concerning his own marriage and the Palatinate, and encouraged him 'by your advices [*sic*] to run the course we are in, with your engagements to the maintaining of it'. He thought little more needed to be said, for 'it is no new business' and 'needs no eloquence... to set it forth'. For this he was grateful as he was 'neither able to do it, nor', he added, 'does it stand with my nature to spend much time in words' (**36**, pp. 28–9). If his message lacked definition, circumstances seemed to lend it urgency. The fighting season was well advanced, yet the English fleet was still not ready to put to sea; and a severe visitation of plague threatened shortly to dislocate his government. Even as he spoke, two more proclamations were being issued, restricting access to London and Westminster (**30**). The case for war, against an enemy yet to be named, could wait no longer.

In political terms, however, Charles was moving too fast, sliding over the relatively modest intentions of the appropriated supply granted in 1624, which, to James's annoyance, deliberately did not mention the Palatinate at all, as well as much that had happened since [**doc. 4 i**] (**28**). A second session of the 1624 Parliament, which might have carried foreign policy collectively forward, had never been held, three times postponed because of difficulties in settling the terms of Charles's French match. During the winter of 1624–25, James, who still set store by diplomacy, had done little to clarify potential war aims. Reluctant to break entirely with Spain, he had nevertheless used – probably improperly – a fifth or more (£61,000) of the appropriated supply to create and maintain an undisciplined English force, drawn in part from the country's jails, under the unreliable mercenary Mansfeld; but on its arrival in Holland he had prevented it taking part in attempts to raise the siege of Breda (**221**). To hurry the French marriage treaty along, he had just before his death agreed to lend Louis XIII a small English fleet, without adequately defining its terms of use. Buckingham, with misplaced hopes of an active military alliance, had by contrast wished to use the ships as a negotiating lever. Charles in 1625 was desperately delaying handing them over, fearful that Louis might send them against his restless Huguenot (that is, Protestant) subjects (**36, 45**). James had already recognised that Louis would need to restore order; but to do so with the help of the English ships would undermine such slight claims as Charles had to be regarded as a Protestant champion after what he and Buckingham imagined was the Elizabethan manner. With some skill the fleet's commander, John Penington, prevented it entering French service until 6 August, too late for it to do political damage while the Parliament of 1625 was actually in session (**36**).

More seriously damaging to Charles's hopes of commanding parliamentary confidence was the French attitude to English Catholics. Primarily for their own domestic reasons, the French proved for once as insistent as the Spanish on relaxation of the penal laws for their co-religionists. This was an acute embarrassment to Charles at a time when he was anxious to stir his subjects against Spain, and to rally Protestant support abroad. In Parliament, it was very likely to give religious issues a prominence he hoped to avoid, and indeed to alter perceptions of his own soundness (**178, 24** *Supp.*).

Only since James's death had Charles and Buckingham been able to make active preparations for the fleet they clearly intended to send out against Spain (**145**). At the same time they undertook to pay £30,000 a month to Charles's Lutheran uncle, Christian IV of Denmark, for intervention on the North German plain where he had territorial and religious interests of his own to pursue against the Habsburgs. Mansfeld, given a chance to help at Breda and then to move on towards the Rhineland Palatinate, was promised £20,000 a month. It was unfortunate that the French negotiations seemed to be yielding so little of promise to the Palatinate cause, for altogether Charles's recent commitments were likely to cost roughly £1 million a year.

Charles never intended that Parliament should shoulder the whole of this sum; but he hoped for substantial supply and for a clear indication, important in foreign eyes, that he carried his

Parliament with him. The emphasis on continental warfare, which these commitments indicated, was not however entirely to the taste of some of those MPs most enthusiastic for war in 1624. For them, far-flung maritime aggression against Spanish shipping and posses-sions – a 'blue-water' policy – was altogether more attractive, and no less likely to put pressure on the Habsburgs. From the general-ities of 1624, the Commons were now faced with the question, not whether they should endorse war, but whether they should support the kind of war which Charles appeared to be proposing. It was one to stir doubts about Buckingham's ascendant role in affairs of state.

MPs had ample opportunity to reflect on these religious and military developments as Charles kept them waiting at Westminster for a month before the session opened, while he strove to settle with Louis XIII. The delay chimed ill with his initial haste to meet Parliament. On the day after James's death he was, according to John Hacket, 'so forward to have it sit that he did both propound, and dispute it, to have no writs go forth to call a new one', but to continue the one adjourned in May 1624, in apparent ignorance – or disregard – of the convention that a sitting Parliament ends on the monarch's death. This had already happened twice under the Tudors. Lord Keeper Williams soon disabused him, according to his biographer Hacket (**18**, part 2, p. 4). Instead, Charles ordered election writs to be sent out at once from Chancery.

In his hurry, or certainty that his case was already carried, Charles neither consulted beforehand with the Court's most in-fluential supporters in the countryside nor engaged again with those Commons leaders, like Sir Dudley Digges and Sir Edwin Sandys, who had been most helpful to him in 1624, although he confined John Digby, Earl of Bristol, to his country estate on his return from his embassy at Madrid. Temporarily, too, his Privy Councillors were thin on the ground in the Lower House, a deficiency made worse by the obvious reluctance of some of them, like Sir Humphrey May, to endorse his case as warmly as he would have liked (**203**). They were reflecting divisions within the Privy Council. Williams, like Arundel, resented Buckingham's monopoly of the King's counsels; and Archbishop Abbot, Pembroke, Lennox and Hamilton all had reasons for coolness. As Sir John Eliot pointed out, for quite long stretches the King's leading spokesman was Sir John Coke, a senior naval commissioner and client of Buckingham, who had yet to be made a Privy Councillor (**36**). On one occasion (8 July) he was backed only by Sir William Becher, the clerk to the Council (**203**). Charles made their position harder by disregarding the convention that the first Parliament of a new reign should have some opportunity to take stock, and made it plain he had little patience with the subtle, but often lengthy, processes by which supply and settlement of grievances went hand-in-hand (**69**). Oddly, he does not seem to have appreciated the extent to which parliamentary leaders of the stature of Sir Edward Coke, Sir Robert Phelips and Sir Francis Seymour might exploit the religious issue (the French match and penal laws as well as unfinished business with Richard Montagu), dwell on grievances not settled in 1624 and take the opportunity to give voice to the growing hostility to Buckingham. Nor did he allow sufficiently for the disruptive effects of Sir Thomas Wentworth's group of 'Northern men', who had already shown their obduracy in 1624 and were again intent on stirring old parliamentary grievances (**203**). In short, he expected obedience, and had not done his parliamentary homework.

The 1625 Parliament was unusual in that it met twice, within a short period but at different locations, as part of a single session (at Westminster 18 June to 11 July; at Oxford 1 to 12 August). In the Westminster meeting, the Commons granted the King two subsidies (roughly £140,000) without strings attached, but without much, if any, relation to the war he was proposing. New monarchs were customarily given an early grant to cover the expenses of their predecessor's funeral and their own coronation. Charles was tempted to let the Commons know he was unhappy at the meagre grant, which Phelips nevertheless regarded as conditional on the performance of the fleet later that summer, and contemplated letting John Coke say so. In the end, he did his best to welcome it (**203**). Tactically, he tried to use the threat of plague variously to suggest an early adjournment or to try to induce immediate additional finance on the grounds of urgent military need. Ultimately, he settled for what may have seemed a clever tactical manoeuvre, based on recent precedent, by which he could give his assent to the new subsidy bill and other useful bills without ending the session, and resume it again at Oxford, still supposedly free from plague, on 1 August (**139**; cf. **104**). It was the first Parliament to meet in that summer month since 1523.

In retrospect, it is easy to see that Charles was likely to encounter nothing but aggravation and frustration in the thinly populated Divinity School at Oxford, with the barrister MPs away on circuit and the House of Lords idle, since the focus was on supply (**23**, vol.

3). The Commons were hardly likely to grant the King further subsidies there (**10**) [**doc. 4 ii, iv**]. To have done so would not have been unprecedented; but because they had twice recently granted supply without conditions, and in 1621 had not subsequently been rewarded with adequate consideration of grievances, a third such grant might unbalance the delicate mechanisms by which they set such store. By concentrating on his war needs, Charles inevitably increased attention on Buckingham (**69**) [**doc. 4**]. The Duke did his best, drawing together support from some of Williams's Commons critics, who tried to push again the ever-present case for a proper appraisal of royal finances, and answering as frankly as he could criticisms of the proposed war and its financing. But Charles's unwillingness to bargain left the mediating MPs stranded (**203**). On 11 August he told the Privy Council that Parliament was about to be dissolved, even though his tonnage and poundage bill was still incomplete, a victim of the lack of bargaining. To the last Abbot and Williams objected; and to his subsequent cost, John Glanville drew up a formal Commons protest just before the dissolution (**16 , 17**).

Charles had shown himself in 1625 to have little natural sympathy with Parliament. He sought supply on his own terms, and did not seriously contemplate redressing grievances. His strategy never commanded the general consent of his Privy Council, and seems to have represented his own preferences and Buckingham's. In the Commons, his Privy Councillors were left to present and defend a case they did not always entirely believe in; and the emergence of John Coke, who was not yet of their number, as a leading spokesman was widely remarked at the time. The Oxford meeting did little more than anticipate the extended attack on Buckingham in the 1626 Parliament, and was upset from the outset at the way Charles appeared to have pardoned a Jesuit at French request just after promising the Westminster session that no further concessions of this kind would be made (**179, 99**). Charles was already beginning to give the impression that he lacked the ability both to manage a Parliament and conduct a war. Twice in 1625, his representatives had hinted that he might have to take other courses and to look elsewhere for finance. In the immediate context of that Parliament, such remarks were intended as ploys to spur on the granting of supply; within a further year, they were to seem to have a more serious meaning (**203**). Charles's long apprenticeship to kingship had not got him off to a happy start in either England or Scotland.

The most recent research suggests that the revisionist claims that Charles was, at the start of his reign, a prince in love with Parliaments, can hardly be sustained (**203, 204**). He seems to have been as casual in his preparations as he was impatient with their formal procedures. MPs for their part undoubtedly attended to the interests of their constituencies; but local sentiment was not the reason for withholding supply. They held back as a matter of political judgement and a concern for the procedures of the Commons, not simply out of sensitivity to local pockets. Neither the nature of the war at hand nor the identity of its directors suggested a sound political investment.

# 4  Parliament, Buckingham and Bristol, 1626

Charles's fleet sailed hesitantly out of Plymouth harbour in October 1625, shortly after Louis XIII had employed the English loan ships against the Huguenots, whose admiral Soubise had fled to England (**45**). The fleet was funded by money the King did not really have, and was ill-equipped to cope with autumnal seas in the Bay of Biscay. Remarkably, all its flag officers were landsmen, some of them with only slender experience of continental warfare: a legacy of England's long years of peace (**11**). Buckingham withdrew at a late stage from its command, and it was led by Sir Edward Cecil, a plain-spoken but perceptive soldier who was not hopeful of success. 'We have all contrary to us, that in respect of such an action may be called impediments,' he wrote to Charles just before he set sail (**83**, vol. 2, p. 143). He produced, nevertheless, the outstanding set of fighting instructions of his day, in contrast to the vague directions he received from the King (**11**). Charles laid almost as much stress on the threat to his 'Dominion of the Narrow Seas, which have been assumed justly by our predecessors, and given to them and us by all our neighbours' as he did on the recovery of the Palatinate (**83**, vol. 2, p. 383). Cecil was to do what damage he could to Spanish shipping, and if possible take a suitable port and capture a treasure fleet. Once off the Spanish coast, he and his Council of War settled for Cadiz, like Drake before them (**17**). Little thereafter went right, as always seemed likely, and almost half the fleet was lost. Some of its sails and tackle had seen service in 1588; but Cecil received only limited understanding, and his men a cold welcome in West Country billets, when they limped home. His departure had been preceded by 'private distempers' within the Privy Council; and neither those who had wanted the expedition, nor those who had not, saw cause to sympathise at its outcome (**5**, 8 September 1625). As a gesture of intent to wavering allies, the enterprise had failed. Cecil's appearance off Cadiz on 22 October had, however, stirred Philip IV into acknowledging at last that Spain was at war with England, a development he did not welcome.

For Charles, Spain's lack of aggression was a problem. His subjects in general were not impressed by the invisibility of the enemy, although the seaboard counties of the south remained apprehensive. Yet even after a false alarm had prompted a hasty renewing of the county of Essex's rotting coastal defences by the Earl of Warwick, he failed to make the most of the Earl's anxiety to impress and only belatedly sent his most trusted agent, and Lord Admiral, Buckingham, to the county to offer encouragement [**doc. 7**]. Charles's cool response, combined with the obvious defensive weaknesses, helped to foster the belief that the King was altogether too eager to provoke a war against a powerful enemy without first doing all he could to ensure his subjects' safety. It was a view soon to be heard in Parliament (**38**).

The persistence of the plague was also inconvenient, keeping the Court away from St James's until the New Year, and disrupting the rhythm of government. Instruction manuals intended to sharpen up the county militias*, for example, had been left behind in Westminster and could not be distributed (**113**). A Privy Seal loan, launched soon after Parliament ended, was coolly received by the gentry at a time of economic depression, and promised little. In October, Buckingham was sent to Amsterdam to pawn surplus Crown jewels, and to the Hague to try to patch up relations with Charles's anti-Habsburg partners (the Dutch, Danes, Swedes, north German princes and French): neither task was easily achieved (**99, 71**). The Dutch may have been reluctant to encourage this venture in extra-parliamentary war funding; but in the end Buckingham managed to raise £58,000 in Amsterdam on the jewels, with the help of the financiers Burlamachi and Calandrini. The French refused to see him (**116, 128**).

Charles accepted that he would have to meet Parliament again very shortly. In preparation, he belatedly carried out his promise to his 1625 Parliament to order the disarming of recusants and, to the Earl Marshal Arundel's evident distaste, for the first time in such instructions specified fourteen peers whose arms he wished to have removed. The provision had the effect of diverting attention away from those unnamed, like the Earl of Rutland, Buckingham's father-in-law, who regularly appeared in the Commons' lists of popish officeholders but in whom Charles clearly had confidence. At the same time, it suggested that those named might be capable of disloyalty; and, in humiliating them, provided a small illustration of Charles's deep-seated inability to trust his subjects. Whether Louis XIII could trust him was another matter; for Charles was now breaching the terms of his recent marriage treaty. More conventionally, in November he also pricked seven of the more querulous MPs of 1625 for a year's service as sheriffs of their counties, thus making them ineligible for the coming Parliament: among them were Sir Edward Coke, who still tried to find a legal loophole, Phelips, Seymour and Wentworth (**99**). On hearing the news, the Bishop of Lincoln, John Williams, now confined to his palace at Buckden after losing the Lord Keepership, caustically observed: 'What then? Am I made high sheriff of Huntingdonshire? Such minute policies are frivolous' (**18**, part 2, p. 70).

Although Charles made some effort in 1625–26 to revert to a more traditionally Protestant foreign policy, it proved to be of little political advantage. Shortly before Parliament met, Louis XIII and Richelieu, fearing war on too many fronts, made peace with their Huguenot rebels, and thus reduced Charles's scope for playing the role of the 'godly prince' (**45**). Moreover, they had not yet returned his loan ships, their use of which cast its own shadow over Charles's Protestant aspirations (**112**, **116**). In Parliament (6 February to 15 June) Charles proved to have little new to offer, and his most urgent plea, now against a background of recent failure, was again for supply. The Crown's critics in the Commons were not against giving, if they could be convinced that the cause was a proper one, in capable hands. But the Cadiz expedition had gone badly wrong, and they had not yet had an opportunity to question the Council of War about the ordering and disposing of the appropriated supply granted in 1624. When they did, in March 1626, they found its members as uncooperative to their probing of war policy as Charles intended: 'It is not you they aim at, but it is me upon whom they make inquisition; and for subsidies.... Gold may be bought too dear' (**5**, 9 March 1626; **221**). Their immediate target, though, was Buckingham.

MPs were also worried at the way in which relations with France, supposedly England's major ally, continued to deteriorate (**45**). From the Queen's new base at Court, French diplomats blamed Buckingham, whom they had long since ceased to esteem, and encouraged opposition to him. Arundel and Pembroke, as well as Eliot and Digges, were among those inclining a sympathetic ear. In recent months there had been serious friction over alleged French trading with Spain. The English and French had subsequently detained several of each other's ships in a spirit of mutual recrimination, to the detriment of the struggling mercantile community; and the Committee of Grievances soon had in hand, through one of its sub-committees under Eliot, an enquiry into Buckingham's treatment of the French vessel *St Peter* of Le Havre. It had been twice stayed, but legally; and the grounds for enquiry were so thin that prompting from the busy new French ambassador, Blainville, seems likely. The case was, however, intended to illustrate the dangers of the Duke's handling of foreign affairs (**178**).

The Commons took up again the question of Richard Montagu's *Appello Caesarem*, after a committee of anti-Calvinist bishops in January had declared it agreeable to the doctrine of the Church of England and had recommended Charles to forbid all further discussion of the disputed points (**213**). As if to pre-empt continued Commons enquiry, but in response to pressure from the puritan peers Warwick and Saye, Buckingham held a disputation on the question of Montagu's orthodoxy at his home, York House, shortly after Parliament assembled. That, too, concluded in Montagu's favour. The Commons committee on religion nevertheless considered that *Appello Caesarem* had violated the doctrine of the Church of England, and had seditiously set King against people and people against one another. But when the House recommended that the book should be burned, Charles merely deplored the religious controversy it had stirred up. His proclamation for establishing the peace and quiet of the Church, of 14 June 1626, was published as Parliament was dissolved. It opposed the 'least innovation', without explicitly stating that Montagu's work fell into that category, although an early draft had done so (**30, 213**) [**doc. 9**]. Calvinist clergy seemed to be left with very little room to manoeuvre; and for the first time in a couple of generations, religion was becoming a major issue again.

From the outset, it was apparent that the new Parliament of 1626 intended to take up where its predecessor had left off, in a way which had not been possible in June 1625. This time, however, members were determined that their grievances should get an early airing [**doc. 4 i**]. Supply was not ruled out, but it was invested with contingency and was not to be hurried [**doc. 11**]. The King's direction of the war did not escape criticism, and Digges and Sir Nathaniel Rich both advocated unlikely schemes tantamount to privatising foreign policy in the interests of the mercantile gentry, whereby an English joint-stock company, operating in the West Indies, could strike at, and tap, Spanish wealth at source (**206**). The main business was to be the role of the Duke of Buckingham in the King's counsels; and in this the House of Lords was to play as large a part as the Commons. In both Houses prominent individuals and groups, like the mercantile puritan peers and gentry, had fallen out with the Duke; but neither House was solidly opposed to him, and his patronage was still considerable and diverse, and included solid Calvinists like Edward Lord Montagu and Sir Robert Harley. Faced with the possibility of Buckingham's impeachment, his remaining clients rallied; and within Parliament there were active elements, working in concert, for his interests, just as there were other groups working against them (**35**, p. 229; **178**; **204**). Both Houses had cause to feel their ranks depleted; but where the Commons made little of the absence of the seven sheriffs, as other Members assumed more prominent roles in proceedings (amongst them Digges, Eliot and Wentworth's ally, Christopher Wandesford), the Lords felt disturbed by the continuing seclusion of Bristol, who had unrivalled knowledge of Charles and Buckingham's more ill-considered dealings at Madrid, but who had not been allowed to sit in either 1624 or 1625. He petitioned the Lords on 22 March for permission to take his seat or to face trial, and succeeded in establishing every peer's right to a writ of summons; but it was not until May that the King was ready to allow him to begin giving testimony in the Upper House, and Charles did so only in the hope that Bristol might be discredited.

Before then Charles, and Buckingham's supporters in Parliament, had to counter two other peers who, directly or obliquely, were moving against the Duke. On 25 February, three days after Eliot had reported to the Commons on the *St Peter* affair, the Lords adopted a proposal from their Grand Committee on Privileges that, in future sessions, no peer should hold more than two of the thirty or more proxy votes usually available from recusant and other peers prevented from attending; Buckingham currently held thirteen. On 4 March, Arundel was sequestered from the Privy Council, and the following day was confined to the Tower of London (**194**). A search failed to find any precedent for a peer being removed during the course of a session. His ostensible offence had been to allow the clandestine marriage of his young heir, Maltravers, to Lady Elizabeth Stuart, for whom Charles had other plans; but his leading part in the Lords' attempt to curb Buckingham's influence in the Upper House may have been decisive, even though the Duke's lost proxies went to his friends. Arundel was close to the Earl of Bristol and had, of course, already distanced himself from the Duke over the breach with Spain (**16**). He had also shown a keen interest in the *St Peter* case. He did not resume his seat until 8 June; and during his absence the Lords went only slowly about the King's business.

Pembroke was another peer capable of standing up to Buckingham; and he too was restless. Sympathetic to Bristol, he had counselled caution over breaking with Spain without the assurance of adequate resources, and he was concerned that there should not now also be a breach with France. He was not aiming to bring the Duke down, but rather to trim his wings, as in the *St Peter* enquiry, and to remedy some of his domestic excesses. Others within the Council may well have agreed with Pembroke; but his clients and friends in the Commons did not necessarily share his moderation. On 11 March, within a week of Arundel's removal to the Tower, and on the day after Charles had asked for immediate supply for 'necessities of state', Dr Samuel Turner, a physician and courtier sitting for Pembroke's Shaftesbury seat, raised six leading questions about Buckingham's role and influence with the Commons Committee of the Whole for Evils, Causes and Remedies. They were immediately taken up, and despite Charles's efforts to deflect the House, formed the basis of the Commons' enquiries until superseded by the thirteen formal articles of impeachment in May (**16**) [**doc. 10**]. Turner's questions were directed at the Crown's impoverishment and the 'evil government of this kingdom', and invited enquiry into the proposition that they were caused by the Duke's lack of competence as Lord Admiral, his monopoly of patronage and his manifestly Catholic family connections. They were grounded, as they had to be in the absence of direct knowledge of the King's inner counsels, 'upon common fame' (that is, general report). The point that Seymour had made on 11 August 1625 – 'Let us lay the fault where it is; the Duke of Buckingham is trusted and it must needs be either in him or his agents' – was being addressed with vigour (**36**, p. 460). Breaking with past practice, the Duke's critics were not charging an otherwise capable minister with a specific mistake, but were accusing Buckingham of a general incompetence which made him unfit to assume so dominant a place in the King's government (**209**). As Charles was aware, they were also implying that he was himself irresponsible in allowing Buckingham too much leeway. Over the next three weeks Buckingham's enemies in the Commons moved steadily ahead with their enquiries into the Duke's role and deeds, setting aside consideration of supply until 27 March (when they approved a motion for three subsidies and three fifteenths). They did so despite rumours that a large Spanish fleet was about to sail north.

On 29 March, the day the House had invited Buckingham to attend, Charles instead summoned its members to his presence. There Lord Keeper Coventry told them that the King could not 'believe that the aim is at the Duke ... but findeth that these proceedings do directly wound the honour and judgement of himself and of his father'. Referring to his foreign policy, Charles added that 'Now ... I am so far engaged ... you think there is no retreat; now you begin to set the dice, and make your own game; but ... be not deceived, it is not a parliamentary way, nor is it a way to deal with a King' (**16**, pp. 5, 6) [see also **doc. 11**]. Charles's lack of appreciation of the intricate relationship between supply and grievances had already been demonstrated anew by Coventry's blunt request for a larger grant, and by his threat of dissolution if a satisfactory answer was not given within three days. On 30 March, however, Buckingham appeared, retracted the deadline, and gave a detailed account of his actions, as well as an unconvincing justification for the King's continuing warlike intentions: 'If you give largely, you shall carry the war to the enemy's door, and keep that peace at home that hath been; whereas ... if you draw the war at home, it brings with it nothing but disturbance and fear' (**40**, vol. 1, p. 226). Unimpressed, the Commons responded with a remonstrance affirming their duty to seek redress on behalf of the common weal for the prejudicial conduct of any of the King's servants (**16**).

At this point, the Easter recess, Charles might have decided to cut the session short. That he did not do so, and let it run on to become the longest of the decade, may well have been primarily because he reckoned that the supply which the Commons envisaged (a further subsidy was added on 26 April, making in all approximately £350,000) came quite close to meeting his actual, and pressing, financial needs, if not the inflated total (over £1 million) he had put before them, which startled many (**69**). There was also the possibility that the bill which would provide for tonnage and poundage throughout his reign, for which there had not been time or sufficient inclination in 1625, might be forthcoming. In practice this omission had yet to cause Charles serious difficulty, although it was hardly 'agreeable to our kingly honour' (**16**, p. 88). After the recess, however, the Commons resolved to lay all other matters aside, as they told Charles when he again urged supply on 20 April. Next day they appointed a steering committee which, spurred still by Turner's questions, proceeded to the 'great business in hand', the drawing up of detailed articles against the Duke. Among its members were Eliot, Digges, Wandesford and John Pym, as well as the travel-weary John Glanville, Recorder of Plymouth, who had been punished for his critical views in 1625 by being sent as secretary to Cecil's Council of War on the Cadiz voyage (**17**).

On 8 May, the articles were ready for presentation to the Lords, and for the first time the Commons openly acknowledged they were impeaching the Duke. Impeachment was an uncertain process, partially revived in 1621 against Bacon and used more fully in 1624 against Cranfield; it was ill-suited to politics and the hidden world in which kings took counsel. In 1626, the Commons did not even charge the Duke with high treason as they might have done in an article added at a late stage, concerning the death of James, in contrast to the sharper proceedings against Strafford in 1641. Whatever the form, however, Charles had no intention of sacrificing Buckingham: 'I myself can be a witness to clear him' in every article, he told the Lords on 11 May (**40**, vol. 1, p. 357).

That same day Charles sent Digges summarily to the Tower for his part in drafting the article which suggested that Buckingham was implicated in poisoning James on his deathbed to ensure he did not hear Bristol's testimony. Eliot went too, after giving an unbridled assessment of the Duke's character and worth during the opening of the impeachment proceedings in the Lords. The Commons halted business until the first of the prisoners, Digges, was released. These were nevertheless unsettling days for Buckingham. He was under pressure on two fronts: from the Commons' articles, and from Bristol's evidence; and he found it difficult to gauge the effect which Bristol, in particular, was having on his fellow peers. By the time Arundel, with his five proxy votes, had taken his seat again on 8 June, after the Lords' Whitsun recess, Buckingham had been charged by Bristol with high treason. Bristol's opportunity had come after Charles had levelled the same charge against him, prompting the Lords to determine to hear both sides of the story. They had, however, for the moment turned down a Commons' request that Buckingham should be placed under restraint during proceedings. Even so, by 8 June, when Buckingham made his formal response to the articles, Charles no longer saw any point in delaying the end. The Lords were not readily going to condemn Bristol (**93, 112**).

On 9 June, the King once more asked urgently for the supply bill, and set a deadline a week hence. The Commons long debated whether to give it a first reading, but preferred, on 14 June, to send a remonstrance against the obstructiveness of the Duke. They gave no assurance that the bill would pass without some redress of grievances, and Charles refused to accept their protest. Instead, he dissolved Parliament the next day, wearied, as he later declared, by the obstructiveness of the Lower House, especially by 'the violent and ill advised passions of a few Members...for private and personal ends' (**40**, vol. 1, p. 410). He might have said that he had been equally stymied by the Lords' refusal to condemn Bristol out of hand. He rejected pleas from Councillors to let the session continue, perhaps reflecting on the lukewarm support they had given the Duke; rather than remove Buckingham from government, · Charles was ready to sacrifice the possibility of supply. Gold could indeed be bought too dear. It remained to be seen, however, whether, as Sir Dudley Carleton had warned on 12 May, Charles would be 'inforced to use new counsels' to raise the supply he urgently needed. Buckingham meanwhile was free to take political revenge on his critics (**40**, vol. 1, p. 359).

# 5 The Forced Loan

As soon as the 1626 Parliament had ended, Charles issued a proclamation forbidding the circulation of its last remonstrance, which he had refused to accept (**30**). Soon afterwards he issued his own *Declaration of the True Causes which moved his Majestie to assemble and after inforced him to dissolve the last two meetings of Parliament* (**40**). Not all its readers may have been convinced by his apologia. It repeated the assumption that support for war had been agreed by Parliament in 1624, and so should have been provided by its successors in 1625 and 1626. It did so despite consistent reluctance by a majority in the Commons to press ahead until they had a clearer idea of the nature of, and immediate necessity for, the war Charles and Buckingham wanted. It also blamed the 'violent and ill advised passions of a few Members' in 1626 for his difficulties in both Parliaments, apparently oblivious of the way Charles himself had undermined that contention (**70**). He had, after all, kept seven of the 1625 leaders out of the 1626 Commons by pricking them sheriff; yet others of similar stature and temper had at once replaced them, making his definition of a 'few' seem unusually elastic, if not deliberately misleading (**40, 79**) [see also **doc. 17**].

Charles and his Council did not immediately introduce a forced loan, but considered other possibilities first. An approach to the City for a loan met a predictably unenthusiastic response, however, and with Crown lands a fast-dwindling asset, Charles's credit-worthiness was in serious decline. A draft proclamation, dated the day after Parliament was dissolved but never issued, proposed that he should appeal to the freeholders of England, through polls conducted by the sheriffs of counties, to support him in collecting the supply he had not received from the 1626 Parliament, where the 'malicious practises of wikked spirits' had got in the way (**78**). A benevolence for the equivalent of five subsidies was launched early in July; but it was making slow progress, as Buckingham began to weed his parliamentary critics from their local offices, when news reached England which galvanised Charles into more thoroughgoing action (**16**).

On 11 September, he learned that his uncle, Christian IV, had been badly beaten by the Bavarian general, Tilly, at the battle of Lutter, and had withdrawn from the main theatre of conflict in order to rally his battered forces. Charles felt this blow to family honour acutely; he was also aware how far he had fallen short in supporting Christian. The obvious course was to recall Parliament. But Charles would have none of it. Then, and subsequently, there were reports that he 'did abominate that name' (**78**, p. 42). Instead he determined, after lengthy debate in the Council, on a new loan – the Forced Loan – at the rate of five subsidies (**16**). He did not leave it to his ministers to take responsibility for this, but from the outset identified himself closely with the levy. It was to be a test of his subjects' loyalty to him at a time when he needed to defend his honour, and he was prepared to polarise the political nation. Gentry who declined to act as commissioners for the loan in the counties were swept from office. Those individuals who held out against payment were informed that Charles 'vows a perpetual remembrance as well as a present punishment' of their neglect, 'for his heart is so inflamed in this business' [**doc. 14**]. Some were imprisoned, with serious consequences for their health. Heavy-handed action was also taken against humbler resisters. In London and Gloucestershire, subsidy men were consigned to service with Christian IV; and seven Chelmsford townsmen won fleeting fame in March 1627 after refusing the press in similar circumstances. After a long Council debate into the evening, Lord Keeper Coventry persuaded his fellow Councillors not to try to impose martial law on them as they could hardly be regarded as mutinying soldiers since they had not accepted press money; this left Attorney General Heath ruefully declaring that 'it had been well if that man had been dead that opened that gap' [**doc. 12**, 14 April]. The seven were never brought to trial; and within days the Council cancelled the threat of impressment for service with Christian altogether.

Councillors, with a few sympathetic peers, spent some weeks in the winter of 1626–27 visiting a dozen counties south of the Trent, in order to encourage support; but there is some evidence that Dr Samuel Turner and other critically disposed gentry were organising a more thorough canvas of their own at much the same time. Many county leaders were faced with an awkward choice between the resistance that the localities expected and the cooperation which might secure Court favour. Sir Thomas Wentworth's solution was to refuse stoutly, but to prove so helpful in confinement that he gained the King's approval [**doc. 14**]. Few were as abrasive as the

Earl of Lincoln (**78**, **99**), but foot-dragging was apparent, even in these unusually tense circumstances [**doc. 12**, 13 April]. As that trenchant observer of his times, the Earl of Clare, noted of two of the more prominent puritan peers: 'Say[e] hath been sick, and is now recovered, is not to be found; Warwick flings to and fro his ships and fixes no where', while for his own part, he 'trudges about his law business, cums not within kenning of court... [nor] neere any of Buckingham's haunts' (**25**, no. 466). The Duke's role in the loan was not, however, a major one [**doc. 12**, 13 April]. He was preoccupied with the series of expeditions launched during these years, and spent much of his time on associated matters at Council meetings. His closest followers provided the firmest support for the King within the Council, but Buckingham himself was not really the loan's architect or principal agent (**79**), and Henry Lord Clifford correctly anticipated that his departure for Rhé would not ease the pressure [**doc. 14**]. Somehow, though, Warwick secured a royal commission authorising privateering activity on unusually favourable terms, very probably through the Queen and his brother, Holland.

Early in 1627, England drifted testily into a wholly unnecessary war with France (**45**). A second expedition had been intended for the Spanish coast in 1626, under Willoughby, but it had to turn back after a few days, defeated by the elements. A subsequent enquiry identified a mass of defects, and suggested that so low was the quality of naval stores that new masts and ropes were as likely to fail as the very old ones still in use (**159**, **167**). From that point on, the Spanish campaign began to recede, helped by attempts from early in 1627 by the Archduchess Isabella in Brussels to bring about peace. There were, however, three more expeditions during 1627 and 1628, all against France. In 1627, Buckingham himself commanded a fleet to La Rochelle, intent on bringing aid the Huguenots were not entirely sure they wanted, since anything which antagonised Louis XIII and Richelieu made a lasting internal settlement more difficult to achieve. His force landed safely at St Martin's on the island of Rhé but failed to capture its citadel and, like Cecil's at Cadiz, suffered heavy losses. It was, however, the last to make landfall. Neither of the 1628 expeditions, a preliminary one with supplies under Denbigh or the main one under Willoughby (after Buckingham's murder), was to manage to break through the French blockade of La Rochelle, or even to inflict serious damage on French shipping. Charles had hoped for more, as by 1627 he was perturbed by French attempts to claim sovereignty of the Narrow Seas, which he regarded as his rightful inheritance. The Palatinate began to seem far away; unlike sovereignty, it no longer had a place in his admirals' instructions.

Hapless though these expeditions were, they brought immense amounts of work for the Deputy Lieutenants*, JPs and their subordinates in the counties. They had to levy troops for the expeditions and for other service overseas, provide them with uniforms and equipment, raise coat-and-conduct money and arrange for their conduct to the port of embarkation. On the troops' return they often found themselves ordered by the Council, at short notice, to find billets for what was left of one or more of the regiments (**197**). Forced billeting, and the friction surrounding it, provided a continual accompaniment to the Council's efforts to collect the Forced Loan (**38, 62**). The application of martial law amongst a civilian population proved a particularly sensitive matter and, even though it was done sparingly, subsequently provoked questions in the Commons about the rights of the subject at a time when the King was also widely believed to be intent on undermining the place of Parliament in the constitution (**63**). Local resentments from time to time boiled over. The freeholders of Essex, a heavily burdened county, adamantly refused the Council's request to help Colchester pay the ship money due from the ports in 1626 and 1627. Finding there was no precedent, the Deputy Lieutenants* and JPs carefully consulted the grand jury* of the county at quarter sessions*, and gained their support. But their action drew a thunderous response from the equally overstretched Council for 'confronting [it] with the counsel and discretions of a grand jury of Essex, as if they and you... had a controlling power over the Acts of State [i.e. Council orders]'. The senior gentry were not abashed, however; and when some of their number took their precedents book up to the Council, it gave way [**doc. 13**].

Essex's reaction was in many respects characteristic. The King's close identification with the loan did not in the event ensure either prompt or complete collection. Apart from widespread late payment, which may well have severely reduced the practical value of the eventual contribution, there was a good deal of bargaining by the Council, allowing the counties to keep loan moneys to pay for forced billeting, or attempting to encourage payment by abandoning claims to ship money. As a result, the Exchequer received less than 70 per cent of the anticipated revenue, although as Richard Cust has shown, the loan raised £267,000 in all (**78**). In financial as well as political terms there was thus a price to pay for the King's short-term 'success'. In the counties, moreover, local governors did much to save Charles from the worst consequences of his follies during the war years, as William Lord Maynard's lieutenancy letter-book graphically shows (**38**). Stripped as they sometimes were of their most experienced leaders by Buckingham's purge, they somehow managed to find the resources to carry through whatever policies the Council expected of them – often several at once – reserving their complaints until afterwards (**114, 197**). Keeping the peace was of paramount importance to them; and although the Deputy Lieutenants'* authority was often called in question in these years, they almost uniformly preserved it. Despite frequent disturbances, there was remarkably little loss of life as a result of forced billeting on an unwelcoming population, even though some of the troops were popish and from Ireland's jails (**114**). By 1629, however, many Deputy Lieutenants* were exhausted, and some were ready to resign. In Parliament and out, the senior gentry, like their Scottish cousins, had by then had a sufficient taste of Charles's methods of conducting affairs (**38**). The loan had renewed fears of unfettered non-parliamentary taxation, evident in 1610, as Charles had endorsed the 'new counsel' of Buckingham and his associates, and succumbed to his own suspicions of Parliament and people. The degree of silent resistance which accompanied its collection provides some indication of the constitutional disquiet felt by the political nation at large.

At the centre, the Privy Council also displayed remarkable unanimity in public, with only Archbishop Abbot hinting at divisions within. At no time did it allow itself to become the rallying point for local discontents. Yet a majority of its members were working for what they saw as a return to normality: the conduct of foreign policy through the Council and in association with Parliament (**78**). They were, however, handicapped by the King's basic assumptions. Because he regarded the loan as a test of his subjects' loyalty, in helping to avenge his honour, he was only likely to consider the recall of Parliament if it met with a ready response. His moderate Councillors, least at ease with the policy, thus found themselves obliged to be as insistent on payment as any of Buckingham's hardliners. It was partly in the interests of future Parliaments that these Councillors indulged in horse-trading with the counties. Several played a tricky game, at times running with the Duke, at others with their more moderate colleagues. It was not difficult to be regarded, as Lord Keeper Coventry was, as two-faced. Occasionally, there were bold strokes, as when the Earl of

Manchester ordered the release of leading loan defaulters from close confinement in the summer of 1627 immediately after Charles had left Westminster for his house at Theobalds (**4**). Charles himself attended the Council less often than he was to do in later years, content to lay down his priorities and to hear his Councillors' views. After all, he expected to be obeyed.

Yet, as financial exigency continued to exert its remorseless pressure, Charles had by the year's end become, temporarily and for the first time, a regular attender at the Council board. To Buckingham's reported surprise, King and Council decided on 29 January to summon Parliament for 17 March, although Charles was still seeking alternative sources of supply [**doc. 15**]. On 11 February he introduced inland ship money at the rate of three subsidies, postponing Parliament for a month; but within days, the easing of pressure on La Rochelle and a City loan for £95,000 persuaded him to withdraw the levy and to meet Parliament after all on 17 March (**199**).

Charles's war policies had borne exceptionally hard on the south-east and the south-west, in a region where Calvinism often found zealous expression. It was thus unfortunate that these same unparliamentary months were also those in which the control of the central administration and policy-making of the Church under the King had moved from Calvinist to anti-Calvinist hands (**213**). Laud, who was already employed in drafting speeches and declarations for both the King and the Duke, had become in effect the most influential churchman in England, although as yet only Bishop of Bath and Wells (**79**). The Archbishop of Canterbury, Abbot, had been suspended from all but his priestly ministry in October 1627 for refusing to license publication of an overly enthusiastic sermon from the ambitious Robert Sibthorpe, advocating passive obedience to the King, and his responsibilities were taken over by a commission headed by Laud and including four like-minded fellow bishops, which remained in effect until June 1628 (**91**). There was much to occupy the new Parliament.

# 6 Parliament and a Kind of Reckoning, 1628–1629

The new Parliament (17 March to 26 June 1628; 20 January to 29 March 1629) met in the shadow of an early dissolution. If supply was not soon in prospect, Charles, with his Council's support, intended to return to prerogative taxation. This was 'a time of action and not for speech', according to Lord Keeper Coventry; and in opening Parliament Charles had denied himself 'tedious...words' in the hope his Commons would avoid 'tedious consultations' (**37**, vol. 2, pp. 2, 3). To encourage a ready response, seventy-six of the hard-core loan resisters had been freed from restraint, and some had stood resoundingly for election, although there was no significant change in the overall composition of the Commons. The Lords had been bolstered by a dozen new peers, and Charles had been assured about their attitude to Buckingham. The Duke and Pembroke were in any case now allies; and Bristol was for the moment absent ill. Charles had warned the Commons that 'if you (which God forbid) should not give that supply, which this kingdom and state requires at your hands...I must, according to my conscience, take those other courses which God hath put into mine hands'. Clumsily, he added: 'I pray you take not this as a threatening, for I scorn to threaten any but mine equals, but as an admonition' (**37**, vol. 2, p. 3). Troops, returned from the disastrous expedition to Rhé in 1627, had spent the winter billeted on the populace as an ill-judged earnest of intent, in a way which had not been found necessary in 1588 (**99**). Coventry's speech had ranged widely over the condition of Europe and, although he did not mention the Palatinate, it was clear that Charles had unfinished continental business to which he must soon attend. The latest relief fleet for La Rochelle, under Denbigh, was even then struggling to make ready at Plymouth. Christian IV, too, needed more support than he was accustomed to getting.

For their part the Commons had matters nearer home on their minds. The repercussions of Charles's recent fund-raising and war effort seemed to demand attention, and many Members were more disposed to contemplate the immediate past than to look ahead to another summer's military activity. Seymour saw other issues as more pressing than supply: 'How shall we know what to give when we do not know what we enjoy since his Majesty is pleased to take what he thinks fit?' he argued early in the session; and Sir Walter Erle, a determined resister of the Forced Loan, was not slow in supplying the heads for enquiry into recent threats to the subject's liberties.

> In the freedom of our persons we have been invaded: first, by enjoining attendance at the Council Board; secondly, by imprisonment; thirdly, by confinement; fourthly, by designing to foreign employments [principally the press for ban-refusers]; fifthly, by undue proceedings in matter of judicature. In the propriety of our goods, by billeting of soldiers, coercive loans and taxes laid by deputy lieutenants* (**37**, vol. 2, pp. 67, 98n–99n).

With some skill, however, the King's Councillors in the Commons managed to secure agreement in principle to a bill for five subsidies (roughly £275,000) by 4 April, after promising to look into current grievances (**79**). They also managed to divert attention away from the Duke, while keeping Charles in the background. His opening remarks had been enough to persuade them that, if possible, he should in future speak through the emollient John Coke, now Secretary of State. On hearing of the proposed supply, Charles cast aside doubts about its adequacy, and remarked that 'he thought he had gained more reputation in Christendom than if he had won many battles'; he professed he was now in love with Parliaments. Buckingham added that 'this day makes you appear as you are, a glorious King loved at home, and now to be feared abroad' (**228**, sig. A; **37**, vol. 2, p. 325). Already, though, enquiries were in train which would retard the progress of supply for fully two months, and which largely subsumed the related issues of the Forced Loan, billeting and other military excesses of the recent past.

One major issue was the way in which the Attorney General, Heath, and behind him the King, had sought to tamper with the records of the court of King's Bench after it had refused bail to five of the knights held in custody, including Sir Walter Erle, Sir John Corbett and Sir Thomas Darnel, in November 1627 (**102, 28, 16**). The five had each sued out a writ of habeas corpus to know the cause of their imprisonment, and had been told that it was by 'his majesty's special commandment' (**102**). This was unexceptional, for it was generally acknowledged that the King must be allowed a degree of discretion. No trial had taken place; the decision was simply a rule of court, governing preliminary procedures, and was thus duly entered in the King's Bench rule book. It was still open to the defendants to try again for bail. Subsequently, however, Heath made repeated efforts to get the clerk of the Crown in King's Bench, John Keeling, to enter the substance of the judges' response to this preliminary plea – that the King's special commandment was sufficient to detain them – on the formal controlment roll of the court, as though it was a verdict after full trial. If he had succeeded, Charles would have secured the precedent for detaining any of his subjects at pleasure. Heath, however, had not managed to overcome either Keeling's uneasiness, or the unwillingness of the judicial bench to cooperate, by the time Parliament began (**102**). Within days, John Selden, counsel for Sir Edmund Hampden, another of the five, had begun to raise on the floor of the House questions about the way proceedings had been recorded, and these prompted a full-scale parliamentary enquiry. In the course of it Buckingham, in defending Heath, revealed that 'the Attorney had a check from the King because he had not entered' the necessary details on the controlment roll (**37**, vol. 5, p. 203).

For several weeks, discussions and enquiries involving both Houses failed to establish a way forward. The majority in the Commons were bent on declaring all discretionary imprisonment illegal, while most Lords and Councillors preferred to allow the King some scope. Charles at first promised to accept a reforming bill, but a month later, on 1 May, went back on his word, and tried to turn the issue into one of trust. Was it not sufficient that he was bound by Magna Carta and the six explanatory statutes which had followed it (**99**)? Yet Secretary Coke had recently admitted breaches of the law under pressure of war. On 2 May, Coventry warned the Commons that Parliament would be dissolved in eleven days' time, and Heath drafted a royal declaration in readiness (**79**, **69**). It deplored the way 'some members of that house [of Commons], blinded with a popular applause, have, under the specious shew of redeeming the liberty of the subject, indevoured to destroy our just power of sovereignty'. They had neglected to give 'so much as one reading' to the supply bill as yet, but instead had 'long debated and, without our privity, concluded upon a declaration of the just liberty of the subject, as they have pretended'. Thus, Charles added in a bitter sentence in his own hand, they had 'deserted us in the time of greatest need, when our dear uncle, the King of Denmark, was put to the greatest distress, when the Rochellors [that is, inhabitants of La Rochelle], being of our religion, were reduced to extreme danger, and the Baltic Sea was brought into hazard of being lost, all matters of no small importance to us and our state'. His honour had again been slighted (**79**, p. 160).

However, Charles withdrew the threat on 12 May, perhaps after early news of Denbigh's failure, which left him needing funds for his main fleet more than ever. By then, the Commons had held a crucial debate on 6 May, which had finally established that they would proceed by way of a Petition of Right. The Petition covered not only arbitrary imprisonment, but also recent excesses by Lords Lieutenants and their subordinates, forced billeting, martial law and forced loans, and reaffirmed the subject's 'rights and liberties according to the laws and statutes of this realm' (**16**, p. 69). Nothing in the Petition was new and its tone was restrained. Like the protestations of 1604 and 1610, it stressed generalised rights and inherited freedoms. It represented the moderate view in Parliament that the two Houses could, and should, act together to secure the rights of the subject without infringing the royal prerogative. It was, however, a petition to Charles as a matter of right, not of grace and favour, and it implied that all actions by the executive ought to be warranted by statute (**112**). Moreover, although the Commons claimed that the King's emergency powers remained intact, and the judges subsequently decreed that they did, the provision for the outright abolition of detention without cause shown suggested otherwise. If granted, the Petition would be enrolled in the law courts, and would be taken into account by the bench when making judgements.

Charles at first gave only a qualified and evasive answer to the Petition, on 2 June; but aware that his supply bill was making no progress as anger against Buckingham grew, he changed his attitude five days later and accepted it in full (**16, 28, 69**). The Commons promptly turned to the subsidy bill again, and in little more than a week sent it up to the Lords. By then Charles had agreed to the publication, in full and unadulterated form, of the Petition and his favourable response of 7 June (**97**). Under the Lords' supervision, 1,500 copies of the two documents were printed ready for distribution at the end of the session. When the time came, however, Charles, with his supply safely secured, chose instead to destroy them all and to substitute a rather bulkier version, which was clearly intended both to muffle the Petition's impact and to assert his own position after having been forced, as he thought, into concessions under pressure. The additional material contained in the version now published included his original, inconclusive answer on 2 June, his speech and subsequent comments in Parliament on 7 June, and his speech at the end of the session on 26 June, when he had asserted that 'none of the Houses...joint or separate...have any power to make or declare a law without my consent', and affirmed his right to collect tonnage and poundage whether or not it had been voted by Parliament. The whole was joined, as a single publication, with the customary end of sessions Table of Statutes, and on the book's title page the Table featured more prominently than the Petition. Charles's action did little to improve his relations with his subjects, or, as it turned out, to diminish the impact of the Petition (**97**).

Before the session ended on 26 June, the Commons had defied the King's instruction three weeks earlier not to hold up the passage of the subsidy bill by embarking, at that late stage, on any 'new business of great length...which may lay any scandal or aspersion upon the state or government or the ministers thereof', by preparing a general remonstrance about the 'miserable' condition of the kingdom, and Buckingham's responsibility for it (**37**, vol. 4, pp. 122, 123). They identified as root causes the recent innovations in religion, which had resulted in undue favour for Catholics like the old Countess of Buckingham, the advancement of anti-Calvinists such as Bishops Laud and Neile, and the neglect of able and orthodox ministers, as well as the innovations in government which had been apparent since 1626 [and see **doc. 16**]. They regretted the King's loss of honour as a consequence of the disastrous expeditions to Cadiz and Rhé, as well as the grievous loss of life, and deplored the decay of trade (**16, 37**). In pressing their diagnosis, they succeeded in securing the impeachment and nominally severe punishment of Roger Mainwaring, one of the clergy who had preached most enthusiastically in support of the Forced Loan, but were blocked by a royal pardon in their attempts to take further action against Richard Montagu (**28**).

In the final days of the session, however, the Commons were seriously disturbed by information which suggested that Charles had sought expert advice about the preparation of a new Book of Rates* (**164**). It was estimated that his annual revenue from customs was already roughly £150,000, with a cut of £30,000 for the much mistrusted customs farmers*. In addition, Bate's case had affirmed the Crown's ability to raise revenues by way of impositions. Not all MPs were merchants, but all were consumers; and they saw the need for urgent discussion of the Crown's profits from trade (**116**, **164**). Such revenues had become a vital source of royal income now that the Crown lands had almost all been sold off; but they plainly also weakened the Commons' grip on supply, and thus on government policy. Such fears doubtless lay behind the Commons' reluctance to rush into a new tonnage and poundage act at the start of Charles's reign, particularly as there had last been an opportunity for major debates on impositions in 1610 and 1614. In June 1628, they only had time to prepare a remonstrance, which reached Charles as he was about to end the session, advising him that, until further notice, levying tonnage and poundage was a 'breach of the fundamental liberties of this kingdom, and contrary to [his]... royal answer to the... Petition of Right' (**16**, p. 73). As he prorogued Parliament on 26 June, Charles declared tonnage and poundage 'one of the chief maintenances of my Crown', and the remonstrance 'so prejudicial unto me, that I am forced to end this session some few hours before I meant it' (**16**, p. 73). Back in 1610 his father, who had begun to appreciate the sensitivity of the issue, had by contrast promised that 'because I find it a grievous thing to impose... I will never do it till I acquaint the Parliament with it' (**37**, vol. 2, p. 380n). Times had changed. The promise had been broken, but the problem remained.

In August 1628 Buckingham suffered his last attack, stabbed at Portsmouth, where the fleet was being prepared, by one of the many servicemen made discontented by their lot in recent years (**145**). His murder caused the postponement of the new parliamentary session from October until January 1629. The King meanwhile took Wentworth into his government and attempted to settle the Church. Soon after the session ended, he had nominated Richard Montagu to the see of Chichester, and in October granted pardons to Sibthorpe, Mainwaring and John Cosin, who had all attracted the critical attention of the Commons, as well as to Montagu. Towards the end of the year, he issued his 'Declaration on the Articles of Religion', which was to form a new preface to the Thirty-nine Articles in the Book of Common Prayer (**16**). It was, in effect, a recasting, at Laud's suggestion, of the Proclamation for the Peace and Quiet of the Church of 14 June 1626, now directed towards strict acceptance of the letter of the Thirty-nine Articles, and thus making it difficult for Calvinist clergy to discuss, for example, Article 17, which dealt with what they regarded as the central, but deeply complex, matter of predestination (**28**). Also in the interests of religious quiet, Charles issued a proclamation on 17 January 1629 suppressing Montagu's *Appello Caesarem*. Montagu by then had made his own peace with Archbishop Abbot, who had been restored to active office during December. Abbot could also have resumed attendance at the Council board, at which Laud and Neile both sat; but he seems never to have done so, recognising that he counted now for little in the King's counsels. For so stout a defender of English Calvinism, it was a depressing conclusion (**91**).

Whatever hopes Charles had for a quiet and profitable second session were quickly dashed. The removal of Buckingham made little difference to the temper of the Commons, who began at once to enquire into the circumstances surrounding the publication of the Petition of Right. Charles tried to be conciliatory; but he was also fretful about his revenues, some part of which was urgently needed by Christian IV who was close to withdrawing from the Thirty Years' War, and he was disturbed at the way in which merchants had begun to challenge his collection of custom dues. He could scarcely contain his impatience, making it clear that he expected a bill for tonnage and poundage to have 'precedence before any other business, to take away all difference which may arise betwixt him and his subjects', and on 26 January getting John Coke to proffer a draft one, unavailingly, to the Commons. Eliot was soon complaining that 'This often iteration of messages doth hinder us more than anything' (**22**, pp. 64–5). He was not, however, much exercised about a bill. Like others, he preferred to probe the ills of the recent past. He and John Selden demanded, as a necessary preliminary to any new bill, further enquiry and debate into the way customs dues had been imposed, and rapidly called on the experiences of the merchant MP, John Rolle, whose goods had been seized for non-payment of duties and who had failed to recover them, despite recourse to the court of Exchequer. In ways like this, they hoped to gain some notion of the present scope of tonnage and poundage and of its relationship to impositions, that similar but more elusive levy. Other Members, like John Pym and Sir Nathaniel Rich, recognised the significance of the enquiries into customs dues, but preferred to give their attention primarily to current difficulties within the Church (**16**). They were concerned particularly to establish the nature of the true and reformed Church of England: they deplored the Arminians' newly entrenched position at the head of its effective hierarchy and, like Bishop Davenant, deeply resented the implication that they were themselves puritans, unrepresentative of the main body of its members [**doc. 16**]. Throughout an untidy session, these two issues ran a parallel course.

In the short term, at least, the customs were to prove the more provocative. Not only was Charles impatient for validating legislation, but he was, as ever, acutely sensitive to any trenching on his prerogative, while remaining determined to exert it to its full extent. When Eliot and others took up again their pursuit of the customs farmers*, on the grounds that these men had acted in their own interests and not in his, the King cut them short by affirming on 25 February through Coke that 'what they did was by his direction and assistance himself in person at the Council table' (**22**, p. 74). He adjourned Parliament later that day in the hope that some way forward might be found. On 2 March, however, when Parliament reconvened, the King knew that resolutions on the state of the Church were imminent, and he therefore intended a further adjournment (**16**). This prompted an unruly, but historic, scene in which two of Eliot's allies – Denzil Holles and Benjamin Valentine – occupied the places of Privy Councillors, who arrived late, next to the Speaker's chair, and held him down, while Eliot presented, in a locked chamber, three resolutions against the enemies of the kingdom and betrayers of its liberties. His targets were the innovators in religion; advisers of tonnage and poundage without parliamentary sanction; and those merchants who voluntarily paid that levy (**28**). Holles, who seemed to know the text well, put the resolutions from beside the chair, and only after they had received some affirmation were the doors opened, allowing Members to stream out. Not all had approved of the conduct of Eliot and his associates; but as Charles afterwards conceded, these 'few malevolent persons, like Empericks and lewd Artists' had, nevertheless, produced arguments which 'easily took hold of the minds of many' [**doc. 17**] (**9**). Once again, by his own account, a few ill-disposed Commons leaders had somehow gained the upper hand in parliamentary exchanges. What Charles does not seem to have realised is that these few were by no means always the same group from one Parliament to another, and that they were more numerous than he cared to acknowledge.

The King immediately issued writs for the arrest of nine Members, including Eliot, Selden, Holles and Valentine, and embarked on a lengthy round of legal argument about the grounds upon which he held them, without legal redress or bail on terms they found acceptable (**174**). Finally the cause was shown as 'contempt and sedition', of such a high and general nature that it could not be easily challenged, and was not what the framers of the Petition of Right had had in mind (**28**). Selden was freed in 1631 at the instance of Arundel and Pembroke, who needed his legal advice; but Eliot, found guilty of sedition in 1631 but declining to submit, died in the Tower in November 1632, his ambition for high office frustrated to the last. That October, Charles had refused him leave to go into the country for the sake of his health, as his plea had been insufficiently humble, and the King subsequently denied his relatives permission to take his body home for burial at Port Eliot. A similar inflexibility had been apparent through all the sessions of the later 1620s, as Charles had shown how ill-equipped he was to manage Parliament while trying to run wars.

# Part Three: Analysis – Personal Rule, 1629–1640

## 7   Government and Order

### The loss of Buckingham

The abrupt dissolution of his third Parliament, followed fairly closely by the end of his wars with France (Treaty of Susa, April 1629) and Spain (Treaty of Madrid, November 1630), gave Charles his first chance to turn his mind to the 'government and order' which he wanted to spread from his Court into all parts of his kingdoms. The recent wars had brought much domestic disorder and cost many lives, more perhaps than Charles realised according to the Commons' Remonstrance of June 1628; but of one death, that of Buckingham, he was, of course, acutely conscious (**37**). He had grown up, politically, in the Duke's company, and Buckingham had helped to give his early government much of its character and shape. Between 1625 and 1628 he had acted as Charles's most trusted adviser and agent, a strong influence on the course of foreign policy, and, for the first time, had been closely involved in a broad range of central administrative affairs (**147**). He had already presided to some effect over the reforming Commission for the Navy between 1618 and 1624, taking the first steps towards reversing thirty years of mismanagement; and Charles subsequently put him at the head of commissions investigating ways of improving Crown revenues in both England and Ireland, and supervising the sale of the last sizeable group of Crown lands (**32, 54**).

Freed by James's death from his need to manage the King's Bedchamber, Buckingham for the first time became a frequenter of the Council board, managing to attend very nearly half the 400 or so routine meetings of the Caroline Privy Council to July 1628, a remarkable total given not only his previously patchy record but also his commitments as Lord Admiral, with a series of expeditions to prepare or to regret, and his periodic absences on special missions [**doc. 7**]. His appearances rarely coincided with those of the King – they seem to have attended together no more than forty or so times, usually when Charles was interested in a shift in policy

– and he seems very often to have been performing in an executive role, pushing an existing policy forward. The King and Duke are much more likely to have acted as a pair at the highly confidential, and unrecorded, 'high policy' meetings of the Council. Only occasionally were there discernible differences of emphasis between them, as over Louis's terms for settling with the Huguenots, or the Duke's scheme for a new gold coinage. While there can be no doubting Charles's determination to assert himself once in power, Buckingham may be regarded as a genuine *valido* or first minister in these years, as well as something of an administrative reformer (**147, 54**). He remained, moreover, more deft than his young master in the arts of patronage. Not only had he ended his differences with Pembroke, but just before his death he had won Wentworth over, much to the chagrin of Sir John Eliot. The most forceful of the 'Northern men' sat in the Lords in the 1629 session, already appointed president of the Council of the North, a transformation so swift that ambition was widely thought to have pushed principle aside (**223; 78, p. 223**)

## Further thoughts of Parliament

The manner of the Duke's death did nothing to still Charles's fear of political dissidence and popular sentiments. He had already shown, in the declarations he issued after the dissolution of his three Parliaments and in the draft declaration which anticipated an early end to the 1628 one, that he was prepared to reduce political issues to a simple matter of trust in himself and to interpret parliamentary contrariness in extreme terms, while giving a simplistic and self-righteous account of his own actions (**79**) [**doc. 17**]. His proclamation of 27 March 1629, 'suppressing false rumours touching parliament', denied its early recall but did not, however, rule out a further meeting when 'our people . . . see more clearly into our intents and actions' and when those ill-affected persons of malevolent dispositions who 'bred this interruption' had received condign punishment (**30, p. 228**). There is no evidence that he ever intended to turn his back permanently on Parliament. Within his Privy Council, debate continued amongst those moderate Councillors who wished Charles to develop his foreign policy in association with Parliament, and in active alliance with the French and his Protestant allies, and those who, in favouring closer links with Spain, rejected the case for Parliament (**172, 39**). By late 1632, it was clear that Charles endorsed the Spanish option; but as

late as October 1633, he still found it necessary to 'so rattle' Lord
Keeper Coventry that 'all thoughts of Parliaments are quite out of
his pate' (**44**, vol. 1, p. 141). He gave some indication of his
current attitude to Parliaments, based on his English experiences,
to Lord Deputy Wentworth as he presided over an Irish one in
1634–35. He referred to the English Parliament as a hydra 'as well
cunning and malitious', best dissolved early, for 'grounded upon
my experience...here, [Parliaments] are of the nature of cats, they
ever grow curst with age...young ones are ever [the] most tractable'
(**44**, vol. 1, pp. 233, 365, and also 353). Inadvertently, Charles also
made plain his basic impatience with, and mistrust of, parliamentary procedure; he was unprepared to reconcile himself easily
to the extended manoeuvring which accompanied the progress of
grievances and supply, and seems to have looked for quick results.
In this light the assurances he sometimes gave that he would allow
a later session to spend its time discussing grievances at length
sound distinctly hollow. The euphoria with which he greeted the
mere promise of supply early in the 1628 session was equally,
revealing of his attitude, perhaps marking the only occasion on
which he genuinely appreciated Parliament's efforts. Expansively,
he declared, 'I love Parliaments. I shall rejoice to meet with my
people often' (**37**, vol. 2, p. 325). The question of what the people
might expect to get out of such meetings was left hanging in the
air.

Nevertheless, in informed political circles in and around the
Court, thoughts of another Parliament were never far away. All
through the 1630s, year after year, there were rumours of an
impending meeting, almost invariably prompted by a development,
or supposed development, in foreign policy (**41**) [**doc. 25**]. It is
a truism that this was a decade without a Parliament, after the
flurry of the 1620s; but it was also a decade in which much of its
politics were conducted with reference to the next Parliament. Just
as Charles and his closest advisers were striving to avoid an
imminent meeting, there were others who did what they could to
bring one about. That earnest Scot, Robert Baillie, in January 1637
saw it as the only answer to problems north and south of the
border; and in the end, interested parties in both kingdoms contrived to do the trick (**3**).

## The Court

The Court was always the central point in Charles's rule. He valued it most as an expression of his kingship, and accorded less importance to its customary role in containing political factions or providing a meeting place for peers and senior gentry from the country. During the 1630s the Court reflected his strongly developed aesthetic sense, his love of ceremonial and his devotion to proper forms. The Order of the Garter, to which he was deeply attached, perfectly combined Charles's preferences. His agents, in common with those from other Courts, combed Europe for artistic treasures, despite the King's limited funds; and Rubens and Van Dyck were among the painters adding lustre to his monarchy. In Van Dyck's case, Charles habitually and apparently arbitrarily reduced his bills before payment. Rubens' panels for the ceiling of the new Banqueting House in Whitehall, commissioned in the late 1620s and celebrating the 'apotheosis of James I', were installed in 1636–37, while the prolific Van Dyck and his assistants, in England for much of the 1630s, presented the royal family and Charles's courtiers with unprecedented elegance (**192**, **153**, **154**). England was very much in the mainstream of European culture. Yet the domestic influence of that culture remains hard to assess (**177**). It is true that many country houses had examples of Van Dyck's work, for he was allowed to take private commissions whenever the King did not need him, and the owners of some of those houses were also receptive to Court architectural fashion. But the extent to which the refined but liberalising culture of Charles's Court, with its insistence on the virtues of peace in an age of religious war, found favour amongst gentry accustomed to a more moralistic, Calvinist culture is open to question (**214**, **192**, cf. **177**). The Rubens ceiling might itself have given pause for thought about developments since 1625. The Court's masques may have offered some opportunity for criticism of the King's pretensions and policies (**186**); but they were seen by few – rarely even by foreign ambassadors – and not all were widely available in print. Stronger comment was to be heard in those London playhouses supported by firmly Calvinist courtiers, particularly during the 1630s when the Queen's circle showed no love for Spain (**15**, **65**).

The Court in the 1630s was a place to which the gentry seldom resorted. Charles, more than any of his predecessors, was determined that they and their families should curtail their visits to London and attend more regularly to their duties and their obligations to provide hospitality in the countryside: recalcitrants were dealt with in Star Chamber in 1632, and Charles personally monitored exemptions thereafter. The gentry, however, were reportedly 'much startled' at the severity of a further order in December 1637, comprising 'the strictest letters which ever came' (**225**, p. 138; **8**, vol. 2, p. 531). Less fortunate folk, afflicted with scrofula, who attended Court in the hope of being touched for the King's Evil* at one of the customary ceremonies each year, found them regularly postponed during the 1630s, especially after Charles's mild brush with smallpox in 1632, sometimes at thoughtlessly short notice after they had travelled long distances (**175**) [**doc. 24**]. For all the passing splendour of his Court, Charles remained a remote and private person (**175**). After years of working within its bounds, one of Christopher Wandesford's kinsmen saw Charles for the first time only when brought formally into his presence on appointment as Attorney of the Court of Wards in 1637 (**44**). Even in the late 1630s, Charles was still reluctant to make his first formal entry into the City of London; and on progress he generally confined himself to royal residences or the country houses of favoured courtiers. Here he attended, in rather solitary fashion, to his responsibilities and spent much time in hunting, and in other relatively private pursuits, within a fairly limited area south of the Trent. The elaborate progresses of Elizabeth may have been a thing of the past; but even by James's standards, Charles seems to have made small contact with the gentry on their country estates. Unlike Elizabeth, he rarely distributed portraits of himself but preferred his subjects to display formally the royal coat of arms. Occasionally, he issued coins bearing hopeful messages about the love of the people being the King's protection (**175**, **167**). But he was always more concerned with making his subjects aware of his kingly office and authority · than he was with securing their affection.

## The direction of government

The Duke's removal from the scene left Charles with full control over his government. Dudley Carleton, now Viscount Dorchester, noted in September 1628 how the King held its 'total directory' in his hands, while leaving 'the executory part to every man within the compass of his charge', a tidy arrangement conditioned, as Clarendon later remarked, by Charles's unwillingness to put any more trust in others 'than was necessary for the capacity they served in' (**5**, 30 September 1628; **7**, vol. 1, p. 62). No minister was allowed to dominate affairs; and Wentworth, who might have done, was made Lord Deputy of Ireland during the summer of

1631. He eventually took up his duties in Dublin in July 1633, having secured prior agreement to eleven 'propositions' concerning his role in Ireland, and to the retention of his post as president of the Council of the North (**223, 129**). Richard Weston, the new Lord Treasurer, became Charles's most trusted adviser, and was accorded unwavering support in the face of concerted attacks from within the Court. As in 1625, Charles made few changes of personnel in 1628–29, and was content to continue to employ the firmly Calvinist ministers brought forward by Buckingham, including Lord Keeper Coventry, Secretary John Coke and the Earl of Manchester, now Lord Privy Seal, as well as Robert Heath until 1634. Not all were high in the King's favour; but the administrative base of the state was always broader than that of the Caroline Church.

Charles made it plain he wanted each of his ministers to deal directly with him, and not to combine with others behind his back either over policy or office. Wentworth's correspondence from Ireland with his ally Laud at Court illustrates how careful Laud had to be about revealing prior knowledge of Wentworth's reports to the King, even though he was anxious to monitor their reception (**44**, e.g. vol. 1, p. 379). Similarly, Laud had to warn Wentworth in May 1638 not to continue to pass off some rough handling of Lord Chancellor Loftus in the court of Castle Chamber in Dublin as the work of the Irish Privy Council when Charles rightly suspected it was the Deputy's own (**31**, vol. 7, p. 432). Wentworth, nevertheless, seldom knew where he stood with the King. At times, he was sent detailed responses which were the result of several hours' work by Charles, aided by Secretary Coke; at others he received cursory letters in the form of instruction without consultation. When one of the latter arrived at Dublin at a crucial moment in shaping foreign policy in February 1637, he took it upon himself, after some weeks' hesitation, to provide Charles with a wholly unsolicited but exhaustive 'memorial' on the grave implications for Ireland of any breach with Spain, aware that its recipient might not appreciate his presumption (**44**, vol. 2, pp. 59–64). The specialist Irish committee of the Privy Council met seldom, and the main body of the Council did not always know very much more about circumstances in Ireland than they did about those in the kingdom of Scotland, with its own distinctive government, which Charles kept very largely to himself. Despite mounting problems there, he did not bring Scottish business to the English Privy Council until July 1638, and then only as a matter of information (**84, 150**). Charles knew a good deal about his kingdoms, and at times was anxious to hear the views of his Council; but he preferred to think, take decisions and compose important letters on his own, often in the Bedchamber, with only Windebank, Coke or Coke's assistant Weckherlin to help. It was not easy for those around him to catch the drift and burden of his thinking, particularly after Weston's death in March 1635. No minister subsequently was as much in the King's confidence (**188**).

There were times, too, when Charles pursued priorities of his own which cut across the responsibilities of the Privy Council or one of his archbishops. His determination to take up his father's initiative for the restoration of St Paul's Cathedral, for example, had unfortunate effects. St Paul's came to monopolise the attention of a newly established Council committee intended to oversee bequests for charitable uses in the country as a whole as part of the reform programme introduced by the Book of Orders* of 1631; and it also caused one of his senior bishops, Bridgeman of Chester, to suffer a humiliating prosecution in the court of High Commission in 1633 on no reasonable grounds (**169**). By 1633, Charles urgently needed £10,000 to start the repair work on St Paul's; and when early that year an unstable and vindictive cleric wildly alleged that Bridgeman had secreted a similar sum from fines collected in his local courts, he at once launched an open investigation within the bishop's jurisdiction. In the process he lost the support of the majority of his Privy Council and did nothing for Bridgeman's standing in a troublesome diocese (**168**). In practice, the symmetry Carleton saw in 1628 became distorted during the 1630s. Charles himself, trusting no one, was constantly involved. As with Charles II after him, his mode of kingship demanded continual vigilance and ensured that he never developed lazy ways.

## The Privy Council

Emerging from Buckingham's shadow, the Council tried during the 1630s to reassert itself as the main source of advice to the King, as well as the key institution in his government. By then, it was well over thirty strong and close to being three times its size under Elizabeth (**1**). It included all the principal officers of state and Household; a small group of Scottish and Anglo-Scottish peers and officeholders; the Archbishops of Canterbury and York and one or two other bishops; a few other peers without major offices; and the two Secretaries of State (John Coke and, from 1632, Francis

Windebank). John Williams, Bishop of Lincoln, had not attended the Council since his dismissal from the Lord Keepership in the autumn of 1625, and by the 1630s was involved in a thicket of litigation in part arising out of revelations he was supposed to have made about Council proceedings. Although the King's presence could draw as many as twenty-five Councillors to its board, its working size remained much as it had ever been, at a dozen or so. It met for administrative business several times a week for much of the year, either at Whitehall or wherever the Court happened to be, overseeing the everyday government of England. During the later 1630s Charles established the practice of presiding over formal meetings once a week, usually on Sundays. The decisions made at all such meetings, although not the discussions which preceded them, are, or ought to be, recorded in its register (1). From time to time it, or one of its specialist committees, was also involved in more sensitive and confidential discussions, usually about foreign policy, from which its clerks were excluded and which were not formally recorded. In the 1630s it had specialist standing committees for trade, foreign plantations, Ireland, ordnance, and most important, foreign affairs. As Charles did not appoint a successor to Buckingham as Lord Admiral until 1638, the Council also supplied the members of the Admiralty commission. Nomination to these standing bodies was for the few: in 1636–37, for example, a mere fourteen Councillors and the two Secretaries supplied their entire membership, and the new Lord Treasurer, Bishop Juxon, alone was on all of them. Arundel and Laud both ·ran him close; and all three were among the six members of the foreign affairs committee. Dorset once drew a distinction between the 'common council', of which he was a member, and this 'cabinet council' whose arcane deliberations were only revealed as and when its members chose to do so. Little is known in detail about the proceedings of any of these bodies; but surviving scraps for the committee on Trade, which did keep minutes, suggest that Charles was a regular and vigorous attender (5, e.g. February to April 1635).

The Council had comparatively few bishops among its members, and only for a short period in 1636 were there as many as three of them together at its board (Laud, Neile and Juxon). Any claim that the bishops exercised undue influence in conciliar government during the 1630s must therefore rest on either Laud's undoubtedly commanding voice at the administrative meetings of the full Council, at which he and Juxon were almost always present, or their strong showing at its standing committees. By contrast, the Scottish presence was a slender one and consisted almost entirely of Scots based in England. Charles himself was erratic in the pattern of his attendances, although overall he sat many more times than his father had done. In the winter of 1627–28, he had presided over thirteen consecutive meetings as he considered the financial alternatives to recalling Parliament – and aroused complaints at the way he had thereby prevented the Council from dealing with matters of private or local interest; and his appearances became markedly more frequent after he had introduced ship money in the autumn of 1634 (**1**). From 1637, he was averaging over forty meetings a year, possibly not far short of James's lifetime total. At these meetings he listened carefully to what his Councillors had to say, but made his own decisions; and once his mind was made up, he was seldom flexible. He revealed again his readiness to identify himself closely and personally with the policies of his government, making criticism difficult.

Freed from the constraints of war and the Forced Loan, the Privy Council in the early 1630s showed clear signs of factiousness, if not of factional divisions, particularly around the person of the then Lord Treasurer Weston (Earl of Portland from June 1633), whose own insidious aggrandising continued despite the economies he had imposed at Court. The Queen, a French Catholic, was amongst those he had irritated; and her circle, which included puritans like Holland, was prominent in opposing the pro-Spanish – and popish – leanings of Weston, Cottington and Windebank. Coventry and Laud were also strongly antagonistic (**193**, **148**). Laud was no friend of Rome; but his attitude owed most to the distaste he shared with Wentworth (once an ally of Weston) for the Treasurer's sluggish and self-serving administration. In correspondence they referred to it by the code name 'The Lady Mora'\*, the antithesis of 'Thorough'\* (**31**, **44**).

## The Council and the counties

It was once fashionable to think of the 1630s as marking the apogee of conciliar power. To view the Council in terms of its capacity to impose its will on the localities is, however, to distort its position. Authoritarian government of the kind to which Laud and Wentworth referred approvingly as 'Thorough'\* had some application to Ireland, but as Laud recognised, never in practice to England (**31**, **95**, **121**) [**doc. 21**]. The Council did not even have a local bureaucracy of its own, and customarily permitted patentees* and projectors* to perform specific services in the localities, sometimes to mutual advantage (**201**). It was, however, always heavily dependent on the readiness of the county gentry to enhance their personal standing by public service as Deputy Lieutenants* or Justices of the Peace (**218**). Once in office, few ambitious gentry were willing to risk terminal loss of the royal favour which had brought about their advancement; and on most occasions they were prepared to cooperate with the Privy Council, providing they were allowed some discretion in adapting its orders to local circumstances (**58**). Such compromises were commonplace, but usually tacit. They meant that the Council rarely achieved exactly what it aimed at; but that it approached its object, more or less closely, without undue prejudice to either government policy or local pretensions. It was a recipe for stable and economical, although uninspired, administration (**95**). So, too, very often was the employment of the common law judges on the six assize circuits, which they rode in pairs twice a year, partly to dispense justice but also to supervise, increasingly reluctantly, the developing round of county administration. They brought with them the full pomp of the law; but, ageing men in poor health that they often were, they could not always resist displays of judicial petulance or of pettishness over the plainness of their entertainment. The Justices of the Peace seem seldom to have attended in the numbers that they ought to have done.

The Council was rarely able to predict the precise nature of the new business which came before it, or do much to control its flow. The King's needs always had priority, and could to some extent be anticipated; but much else came in unsolicited fashion, especially by way of the unending stream of personal and local petitions from individuals and institutions which had to be sorted, considered and acted upon. Charles, to whom many were addressed, had little to do with them, especially those which had to be rejected. Like most monarchs he was anxious to be regarded only as bountiful. The Council registers give some impression of how various the nature of Council proceedings often was, and of the way in which Councillors had to work hard to refresh their collective memory of the details of long-running cases whenever these next came before them (**1**). The internal arrangement of the registers suggests that Council clerks were slower than their counterparts in local Church courts in making routine use of cross-referencing, perhaps because they found it hard to develop common practices during their short tours of duty. Nevertheless, one of the most notable characteristics of the early Stuart Council is its perseverance over an extended period with quite minor matters, even during times of high social and economic tension, in pursuit of an agreed and lasting settlement. Through the worst of the crisis of 1630–31, for example, when it had much else to do, it patiently let a hard-fought tussle run its course between the city of Chester and Sir Ranulph Crewe (former Chief Justice of the court of Common Pleas, dismissed by Charles in 1626 for refusing formally to endorse the Forced Loan) over rights to the tolls on the city's Eastgate. It was rewarded by a twenty-one-year agreement between the parties, which in due course was renewed for a second term (**1**, from 9 June 1630).

Another of the Council's characteristics, typical of its day, was that it seldom looked very far ahead, but that, under pressure of business, it confined itself to responding to immediate circumstances. These might include a severe visitation of plague, a failed harvest, or the threat of serious disorder after trade had slumped; sometimes those all occurred together, as was the case in 1630. The books of orders* the Council sent out that year, providing instructions to JPs for dealing with both plague and dearth, were typical of its responses: they had been issued, and revised, several times before, and were thus known to be relatively effective; and they addressed an immediate, and short-term, circumstance (**190**). The more celebrated Book of Orders* of January 1631 was, however, different, springing from individual initiative, reviving a still-born Jacobean precedent, not wholly or primarily addressed to the prevailing crisis, and introducing the notion of continual reporting by the county JPs to the Council about a range of routine local circumstances for the indefinite future. The assize judges were to act as intermediaries. Charles doubtless appreciated how such a scheme might reflect favourably on his kingship while bolstering his hopes for 'order and government'; but the credit for its introduction more properly belongs with its progenitor Francis Bacon, its reviver Edward Cecil (now Viscount Wimbledon), and its mentor in 1630–31, the Earl of Manchester (**169**). Its impact was mixed and, as much of its procedure was based on existing local practice, aroused only limited attention in many counties. In others, however, such as Lancashire, it helped bring administrative practices into line with those favoured by the majority elsewhere, and had an enlivening effect on county government. Nowhere, however, did it bear unduly heavily on the JPs, for it was emphatically not an English expression of 'Thorough'* (cf. **58**). Only a fraction of the supposedly regular reports were ever returned; but as it was, the Council had no time to digest them, especially after the introduction of ship money in 1634, and never looked like establishing any kind of dialogue with the counties about their returns. As Wentworth had once complained in a similar context, this lack of response from the centre – however unavoidable – was no stimulus to further activity or to accurate reporting. It also contrasted with the trouble the Council took over suits and petitions.

At best, the Council was capable of dealing with only one major issue at any one time (**114**). Between the crisis of the early 1630s and the introduction of ship money, the military reforms which Charles had first sought in 1625–26, and brusquely stirred again in September 1628, faltered and were virtually lost. New statutes regulating arms assessments and attendance at musters, which the Lieutenants* sorely needed to replace the outmoded Marian ones, had not been forthcoming in the Parliaments of the 1620s, leaving them dependent on conciliar authority (**191**). Yet the Council was so hard pressed that, however willing, it had little or no time to spare for such basic and necessary tasks as disciplining those members of the trained bands* who missed musters. It did what it could; but especially in more distant counties, the Deputy Lieutenants* were not disposed to send men up since the procedure, by which the defaulters registered their appearances at the Council, spent some days in custody and were then sent home after a formal reprimand, caused them to be away from work for far too long (**1**). The punishment did not seem to fit the misdemeanour. In consequence, only hardened offenders were reported; and others knew that only minimal attention to duty was necessary to avoid trouble. What was needed was a statute enabling Lieutenants* to punish defaulters on the spot (**191**). In such ways were Charles's hopes for a perfect militia undermined.

Ship money dominated the Council's proceedings for most of the later 1630s, as scores of obstinate local rating disputes found their way upwards, obscuring its view of other pressing matters. By concentrating once more on a single issue, the Council did much, by persuasion and compromise as well as discipline, to raise the high totals eventually collected between 1635 and 1638. But those totals also undoubtedly owed something to the identity of the policy with the person of the King. Charles took to interviewing at its board those sheriffs of southern counties who were lagging in their collections; and some, like the incorrigible Sir Humphrey Mildmay, made regular appearances (**170**).

More generally, Charles was never as interested as James had been in the processes of English government, and was more concerned with bringing Scottish practice into line than with making changes elsewhere. In Scotland, he had, for example, followed his revocation of 1625 by tidily rearranging the membership of both the Scottish Privy Council and the Court of Sessions (a civil court), excluding lawyers from the former and trying to exclude peers from the latter. Deprived since 1603 of a royal Court, his Scottish nobles had little enough to do as it was (**150**). The 'government and order' emanating from Whitehall was not always suffused with regal light. By late 1637, there were signs that Charles's control was breaking down at Court itself [**doc. 28**].

# 8  The King's Finances

## Basic problems

The recent wars had cost Charles dear. Even though Parliament had, for all its reservations, granted a total of twelve subsidies between 1621 and 1628, and the King had levied the equivalent of another five through the Forced Loan of 1626–27, he found himself by 1629 roughly £2 million in debt. His scope for manoeuvre was limited. Relations with the City of London were already strained, especially in the case of those aldermen with a concessionary interest in foreign trade who were faced with paying tonnage and poundage, still unratified by Parliament, rather than farming it as some of the domestic concessionaries did (**48**). Even if he had the collateral, he was hardly able to use it as a source for further loans while a scheme for repaying earlier ones slowly worked itself out. Introduced in 1627–28, the scheme authorised the City to sell over a number of years, for the King and also on its own behalf, much of what was left of the Crown lands, thus bringing to an end the traditional means by which the medieval monarchy had under-pinned itself. Philip Burlamachi, the financier who had contributed most to the private funding of royal policy during the 1620s, was by 1629 so enmeshed in the tangled web of Caroline finance that he was shortly to be brought down, and bankrupted, when Lord Treasurer Weston failed to honour a verbal promise to repay some of his moneys in 1633 (**50, 49, 51, 128**). In 1629, the King's regular, or ordinary, annual income amounted to just over £600,000 a year, more than one-third of which was spent on maintaining the royal Household and its establishment of 1,700. The absence of parliamentary supply for the immediate future was thus not Charles's most pressing problem, for that was normally reserved for extraordinary occasions, and did not contribute to the King's ordinary revenues. Much more urgent was the need to increase the level of his annual income and regulate more closely the ways in which it was spent. Fundamental reforms of an antiquated system were out of the question, if only because early seventeenth-century kings and ministers tended naturally to look backwards rather than forwards, and to think in terms of removing impurities from a once healthy body, instead of changing the structure for a new one.

A series of commissions under the Great Seal enquired into the major spending departments like the Household, Navy and Ordnance Office, as well as central and local courts; but although they stirred a certain amount of dust, they were thwarted by the vested interests of powerful men, and achieved little. Household expenditure actually rose in the later 1630s, as though the occasions for fraud had merely been shifted around, not removed (**53**) [**doc. 28**]. The commissions on fees, revived in 1627 and renewed several times, found it difficult to reconcile the need, in the interest of the subject, to reduce charges made by the courts for administrative processes with the King's need to create revenue by fining holders of offices which, in effect, allowed those fees to remain high. Before he died, Weston had contrived to reduce the Crown debt to £1.16 million; but it was clear that an economy drive, in a context in which the concept of inflation was not understood, was unlikely to be sustained.

The customs, however, held out more hope. They had long since become a staple constituent of the ordinary revenue of the Crown; yet four years into the new reign they still lacked their customary validation, and definition by parliamentary statute. Even though trade recovered only slowly from the stoppages over tonnage and poundage in 1629–30, the revenue from this source between 1631 and 1635 amounted to about £273,000 a year, more than one-third of Charles's ordinary income (**53**). The amiable and unobtrusive Bishop Juxon, rather than the commanding Wentworth or the ever-eager Laud, became Treasurer in March 1636 after the Treasury had spent a vigorous year in commission following Weston's death. He increased the income from the farms of the great and petty customs which were put in the hands of new, courtly syndicates headed by the Queen's servant Goring, and, using a new Book of Rates* (1635), raised the duties on a wide range of commodities. He also exploited much more fully the opening given to the Crown by Bate's case in 1606 to levy new and additional impositions. In the later 1630s, annual returns from trade averaged £425,000, almost half the Crown's ordinary revenue. With higher annual returns from other sources, such as the Court of Wards where revenue increased by one-third to £75,000 through more effective management, and the unpopular and 'popish' soap monopoly, which brought in £33,000, Charles's ordinary income towards the end of the decade rose to £899,000 a year. Meanwhile Ireland, under Wentworth's forceful management, had grown to self-sufficiency and ceased to be a burden on the English Exchequer.

Such a revenue might be thought to have left Charles in a comfortable financial position. In practice, however, he remained under severe constraints. The avenues by which he could raise money were narrowing. Burlamachi had gone by 1633; and the City was for the moment an unpromising prospect. Only the customs farmers* were available (**50**). Moreover because of limited sources of immediate funding, the Crown increasingly was obliged to anticipate its income, in effect spending a proportion of it before it was received. By 1635, almost two-thirds of Crown revenues were being anticipated in this way, and Charles was heavily dependent on the customs farmers*, in their role as financiers, to provide contingency funding. Anticipations bypassed the Exchequer, depriving the officers of receipt there of control over expenditure, since they could only operate effectively if all receipts and payments actually passed through their hands, as they repeatedly pointed out during the later 1630s (**49, 50**). More seriously still, much of the additional income generated during the 1630s came from sources which a future Parliament would almost certainly declare illegal as soon as it met. For that reason as much as any other, Charles was committed to putting off its recall for as long as he reasonably could [cf. **doc. 25**].

## Distraint of knighthood

To give his finances some early bolstering, and with Attorney General Heath's help, the King took up in 1630 the hitherto neglected opportunity to impose a fine on all those of his subjects regarded as eligible for knighthood who had spurned the chance to receive the honour at his coronation (**144**). At the time, Charles had refused to contemplate making any new knights on the grounds that there were too many of them already. He subsequently revised his opinion; but there was no question of new creations now. Altogether a total of £174,284 was raised, mostly by 1635, from 9,280 individuals – mainly peers, baronets, esquires and gentry, but including some yeomen and husbandmen, too – who had held land to the annual value of £40 for three years at the time of the coronation but who had neglected the formal obligation to be knighted. Some fines on recalcitrants were undoubtedly punitive, but much of the revenue came from small payments at the minimum of £10; and many whom later generations supposed had resisted, like John Hampden and Oliver Cromwell, paid without apparent demur. Sir Robert Phelips, who as an MP during the 1620s had kept a close eye on Crown finances, was among his county's commissioners, and Wentworth, who had stood out against the Forced Loan, was an extraordinarily effective collector in Yorkshire. But among the peers who did not pay were Arundel, Essex and Saye. Despite a good deal of quiet evasion, distraint was largely successful for three reasons: it was legitimate; it was a matter of indifference to that important part of the political nation which was knighted already; and it tapped the wealth of those notoriously elusive groups of professional men in London, who supplied only one-fifth of the payers but approaching one-half (over £70,000) of the total receipts.

## Royal forests

The royal forests also provided supplementary income during the early 1630s; but they did so from a source sorely troubled by the Crown's policy of disafforesting its smaller woodlands, which provoked riots in the south-west, and of exploiting natural resources within major forests like Dean (**184**). The management of the forests had long been inadequate; but Weston's plans to revive the machinery of the forest courts and restore traditional bounds were upset by the increasingly serious illness of Attorney General Noy (**127**). When, before the first proceedings in the Forest of Dean (always particularly associated with timber for the Royal Navy, as in Armada years), Sir John Finch was appointed to take Noy's place as Crown counsel, the implementation of the policy was largely in the hands of Weston's critics in the Queen's circle; for Holland was Chief Justice in Eyre south of the Trent, and thus presided with two common law judges over the chief forest court, the court of Justice Seat (**103**). When the Justice Seat met in Dean in July 1634, the forest's bounds were held to extend far beyond their current limits, according to an 'undated document of unknown provenance' which Finch, without qualms about its authenticity, produced in court. As a result more local gentry incurred fines for encroachment than might have been anticipated. In addition, a group of prominent lessees of the royal ironworks there, who happened to be Catholics or associates of Weston, were found guilty of despoiling the King's timber for their own purposes. Finch did not hesitate, as ship money was being launched, to call to mind rumours of popish designs on Dean in 1588 [**doc. 23**]. He and Holland both appreciated the King's need for funds, and throughout the proceedings which followed in the other royal forests, revenue-raising appeared as important as administrative improvements.

In forests where there was no clear 'popish' interest, Holland played a different game, as if to suggest that Weston's basic policy was itself badly flawed. Thus at the Justice Seat for Waltham Forest in October 1634, his puritanical brother Warwick was given an opportunity, in defence of the subject's property rights, to clash hard with Finch over his interpretation of its boundaries and, with the grand jury*, to challenge the authenticity of his latest ancient, and closely guarded, evidence (**5**). That a number of the major landholders in that forest happened to be Catholic themselves was, for Warwick, beside the point for the moment. Overall, Holland seems to have made enemies for himself at Court without gaining much revenue for the King. Many of the swingeing fines on landholders within the royal forests of Dean, Waltham and Northamptonshire were later reduced; and the total sum raised for disafforestation there, after much ruffling of gentry feathers, was no more than £38,667 (**163**). In addition, the courts had imposed many hundreds of very small fines on humble folk for minor indiscretions in the forests, some stretching back over ten or twenty years; their attendance, as Edward Lord Montagu remarked, obliged them to miss a day's work they could ill afford to lose (**23**, vol. 3, p. 371).

## Ship money

The largest, and politically most important, additional source of revenue was ship money. Its origins lay in an ancient right of the Crown to levy ships from subjects in coastal towns in order to protect the commonweal during an immediate, short-term emergency; once the danger had passed the ships were returned to their owners (Thrush in **225**). The levy had no set form, at times being ostensibly voluntary (as in 1602), and sometimes involving money as well as ships. Ship money during the 1630s was different. It was intended to sustain the King's own fleet, and to give Charles the chance to mount a diplomatically active foreign policy outside Parliament, while at the same time asserting his sovereignty over the British seas. It was almost entirely a fiscal levy, and only London provided ships rather than money; but almost all the receipts were applied to the Royal Navy or to related purposes, and none of the money was absorbed into the King's ordinary revenues. It was unusually heavy in its demands, and it continued year after year; for once introduced, it was not to be easily given up, although the sums asked for might vary. Charles never found a satisfactory alternative source for the substantial, regular funding his Navy desperately needed, and now, for the first time, received (**166**). A sense of continuity was inculcated by the way the writs for the next levy were usually issued some time before collection on the current one was complete. Restricted in its first writ in 1634–35 to coastal shires, ship money was extended in later ones to all counties, as had been widely anticipated, and realised altogether an unparalleled sum in excess of £800,000 out of the £1 million assessed on England and Wales in six annual levies (**16**). The Navy, which had much to put right, had never been so well supplied (**47, 166**). On the first three writs annual arrears ran at less than 4 per cent, and only in 1639–40 did they exceed 20 per cent. Payment was rarely made with the speed the Council expected, however, and, as with the City of London, cooperation was not always wholehearted (**100, 49**).

Ship money was raised in the form of a rate, and not a tax. This was appropriate, as the need was a specific one, and could be costed. The total sum required was thus predetermined (in 1635–36, the peak year, £215,700; in three of the four later years, £210,400); and the Council then imposed on each county and corporate town a lump sum calculated according to a rough estimate of its comparative prosperity. Within each county the high sheriff was made solely responsible for arranging and making the collection. Such a method was crude but effective (**100**). Where possible, the sheriff and his assistants made use of existing rating schemes, right down to parish level, as the basis of taxation widened dramatically: in Essex, for example, 330 individuals (including 188 'Londoners') had been distrained for knighthood, and 3,700 had paid the subsidies of 1628, but no fewer than 14,000 were assessed for ship money in 1637. The unprecedented weight of the sum demanded (close to three subsidies a year) almost inevitably exposed the flaws in parish and hundredal systems normally used to collect a few pounds. Rating disputes were thus very common, and the more stubborn of them took up much Council time. Distraint for non-payment followed, sometimes accompanied by violence. How far such disputes in themselves reflected stirring of constitutional unease about the continuing levies, rather than a simple wish to delay or avoid payment, is open to question; but there is some evidence that disputants hoped to block levies by clogging up Council proceedings altogether. As it happened, Charles's frequent appearances at the Council may also have slowed the progress of its routine business. Even so, the Council again found opportunities to exercise those bargaining skills, which it had already displayed over the Forced Loan, with individuals and communities prepared to stand up for themselves (**138**).

What is clear is that pressure at Court, following the collapse of his pro-Habsburg foreign policy, had convinced Charles by February 1637 that he needed to clarify and assert his right to collect the rate in order to secure the funding for his Navy, and to ensure his continuing freedom to determine foreign policy. Hurriedly, and shortly before the assize circuits, he referred a statement of his constitutional position to the twelve common law judges for their opinions. Their deliberations were to be supervised by Sir John Finch, who was now Chief Justice of Common Pleas and the King's intermediary with the bench. For the nine puisne or junior judges, this was their first chance to express a view; and all twelve were expected to do so without having the benefit of counsels' arguments or, indeed, hearing much of each others' thoughts in advance (**16**). Charles wanted their support for his assertion that he had a right to levy money from his subjects for the benefit of the whole commonweal in emergencies, and that he was the sole judge of what constituted such an emergency. As ship money was then entering on its fourth levy at a time when Court poets were acclaiming England's uniquely peaceful condition in a warring Europe, the current emergency was clearly of an elastic, and to many an invisible, nature. Crises, and states of emergency, after all were normally widely apparent, and were seen to run their course more or less quickly. These points clearly troubled a number of the judges during their discussions, and with the veterans Croke and Hutton adhering to hostile views they had already made public, only a bare majority truly supported the 'unanimous' approval they gave, after careful debate, to the King's case. Unanimity had been achieved only by observance of the convention that the minority should fall in, at the last, with the opinion of the majority (**126, 165**).

Nevertheless, Charles predictably made much of the judges' unanimous support for what Laud had thought would otherwise be a 'very dead horse' (**31**, vol. 7, p. 364). The response of Charles's subjects was more considered, and more apprehensive. Few accounts survive of reactions to the addresses in court by the judges on the assize circuits which shortly followed; but after the Exchequer judge, Weston, had spoken at Maidstone, Sir Roger Twysden, a Kent JP always deeply interested in the processes of government, took detailed note of the local response. While some of Weston's hearers were still prepared to accept the King's case, many others were, like himself, disquieted by the absence of an obvious emergency, and deeply worried about the consequences of the judges' opinion for the future of Parliament (**90**) [**doc. 26**]. They also regretted that the levy had now lost even the illusion of being voluntary, and that the sense of helping a monarch in genuine need, apparent under Elizabeth and James I, had gone. Their freedom to do what they would with their property was thus being curtailed. Such manor-house deliberations could have no ready outcome; but they echoed, probably unknowingly, the reservations felt in private by at least a minority of the judges (**90**).

Either unaware of the bench's misgivings, or ignoring them, Charles now pressed ahead with preparations for a full-blown public trial of a leading resister. He was determined to speed up the rate of payments, as lateness, in the case of a levy intended for immediate application, was a potentially crippling shortcoming. The subject of this test case which, at length and at last, would publicly demonstrate the legality of the King's claim to ship money, was the Buckinghamshire squire John Hampden (**28**). Hampden had sat in all the Parliaments of the 1620s and had influential friends among the critics of ship money, from George Croke to Viscount Saye, but was not then himself as prominent as he was to become. Saye, who had begun a ship-money action of his own in King's Bench against the Crown and was very anxious to be the subject of such a trial, was carefully ignored (**57**). Public concern was again widely apparent. For this, said Twysden, 'was the greatest cause according to the general opinion of the world... ever heard out of parliament in England' (**90**, p. 234). According to Robert Woodford, a godly steward from Northampton then in London, when early in November 1637 Oliver St John opened Hampden's defence in Exchequer Chamber – where on Hampden's demurrer it had been adjourned from the Exchequer – 'he was much applauded and hummed by the bystanders, though my Lord Finch signified his displeasure for it'. So satisfying was St John's argument, that at its close they 'adventured to hum him againe' (**20**,

p. 496; **16**, **89**). Later that month, Thomas Knyvett, a Norfolk squire up in town, rose 'by peepe of the day' to hear the King's case opened, but was disappointed to find he could get no nearer to the door of the court than 'two or three yards, the crowd was so great' (**42**, p. 91).

Once counsel on both sides had argued their cases by mid-December, the presiding judges referred the whole matter, as one of outstanding importance, to the entire bench for individual decisions. In pairs and starting with the most junior, Weston and Crawley, the judges delivered themselves at length over the following six months. By mid-April 1638, the Crown had a 5-to-1 advantage, with only Croke dissenting; but thereafter it was a close-run thing. Hutton and Denham both found against the Crown. Crucially, Judge Jones 'fluttered in his argument, meteor-like hung between heaven and earth, and yet in the end concluded against Mr Hampden' (**20**, p. 497). In his flutterings he had, however, probed a potential weakness in the Crown's case, concerning the handling of ship-money revenues on receipt. They should, he argued, have gone into a separate fund, not to the Treasurer of the Navy, for although the King might command the service, he did so on behalf of the commonweal and could not receive the money himself. It was a technical point, and Jones gave the government the benefit of the doubt. But it enabled two of the three chief judges, Bramston and Davenport, who had been uneasy all along but were now hamstrung by the unanimous acceptance of the case back in February, to identify and sustain grounds, narrow and technical though they were, by which they might argue against the Crown in this instance (**180**). They directed their attention more certainly than Jones had done to the way in which the levy had been carried out and, unlike him, concluded that the Crown had not acted in a wholly proper manner. Sir William Russell, Charles's Treasurer for the Navy, had indeed received and disbursed ship money. Finch provided the seventh voice the Crown needed; but the majority could not have been slimmer. Hampden was guilty, but only just. It fell to Chief Baron Davenport, as presiding judge, to deliver sentence on behalf of the Court of Exchequer. That he had himself been one of the large dissenting minority did nothing to reduce the hollowness of the Crown's victory. Unlike Croke and Hutton, however, Davenport and Bramston had fired no imaginations, and won few friends, for contemporaries do not seem to have fully appreciated their efforts, in difficult circumstances, to limit the King's discretion and to protect the subject's property (**126**). For its part, the Crown could use the verdict to block actions like Saye's, but had been denied the political triumph Charles wanted. How much Finch had told him of the judges' unease in February 1637 is uncertain; but either wilfully, or in ignorance, the King had, while pursuing Hampden, lost much of his earlier advantage. Like the trial in Scotland at about the same time of Lord Balmerino for spreading slander against the Crown, which went ahead on patently shaky ground, it was a mess Charles ought not to have allowed himself to get into. That he did says much about his determination always to be proved right (**14, 84, 150**).

By the time Hampden had been found guilty, in June 1638, attention at court and in the country was turning to Scotland, where Charles's intention of establishing religious conformity according to English practices had met with stubborn resistance (**84, 150**). His new canons, and more especially the final, and much-delayed, version of the new Scottish prayer book, had provoked outraged – and unconsulted – nobility, gentry, burgesses and clergy to launch a national covenant at the end of February 1638, which had been gathering support ever since. As Laud privately disclaimed responsibility for the turn of events, the covenanters looked to England for joint Calvinist action against the impurities of Arminianism at the centre (**3**). Like Charles, they were preparing for the possibility of war. It was not a prospect the English as a whole viewed with any enthusiasm, although it promised to bring Parliament nearer. The final, fading, ship-money years suggest as much. The 1638–39 levy, despite being levied at only one-third the normal rate, nevertheless ended with arrears of almost 20 per cent, well over twice the percentage in the preceding year; and the final levy, in 1639–40, was ignored by 80 per cent of those rated (**100**).

The King's need for funds was thus more acute than ever. After a first, indecisive venture north, Charles in October 1639 appointed a Council committee to consider his financial prospects. Even those of its members most averse to the idea 'did now begin to advise the King's making trial of his people in Parliament' before any further resort to prerogative supply [**doc. 30**]. Like the Council as a whole, Charles recognised the force of the advice and rapidly agreed. Only Parliament could provide the funds for an army. Charles had benefited from the Continent's preoccupation with war during the 1630s; but he had failed to ensure peace in his own back yard. No matter where the threat of war arose, however, his fragile finances could not cope with it.

# 9 Foreign Policy and the Navy

The peace treaties which Charles concluded with France (Susa, April 1629) and Spain (Madrid, November 1630) brought recent humiliations to an end, but did nothing for 'that...unfortunate knotty affair of the Palatinate', as James had described it back in 1623 (**227**, p. 241). Neither contained any undertaking to help in its recovery, the prospects for which had recently been weakened by the withdrawal of Christian IV, who had wearily made his peace with the Emperor in May 1629. The French treaty was little more than a resumption of superficially friendly relations, with a tacit agreement between the two kings not to interfere with each other's subjects; Louis made no claims for English Catholics or for his sister, Henrietta Maria's, household. The treaty with Spain was similar to the Treaty of London of 1604, and ended Charles's early hopes of wringing at least a minor concession on the Palatinate from Spain (**39**). Instead, Cottington, who had negotiated the main treaty, went on to conclude with Olivares a secret agreement in January 1631 by which the English would join with Spain in attacking its rebel Dutch subjects by land and sea and, when successful, partitioning the United Provinces between them. This latter treaty was never ratified, and stood little chance of being implemented, since Charles, for all his reservations about the Dutch, was not anxious to crush his closest Protestant neighbours with whom his countrymen had many ties and whose help he might still need. But it provided some indication of his readiness to join with Spain, and was to serve as a durable point of reference for Anglo-Spanish discussions throughout the 1630s.

Discussions, as much as serious negotiations, epitomise Caroline foreign policy during the 1630s. There was continual diplomatic activity, and in the early 1630s strenuous conciliar debate, but little action, even after the rehabilitated fleet took to the seas in 1635. The French made a number of efforts, in concert with the Queen, Holland and Carlisle, to press the case for an English foreign policy undertaken with the support of Parliament; but the francophiles had lost the initial argument within the Council during 1632, and although hopes revived in the winter of 1636–37, they had to settle for a relationship based on diplomatic familiarity rather than military action (**172**). As Richelieu once remarked, it was politic to maintain inconclusive negotiations 'with persons with whom it is always necessary to negotiate' (**171**, p. 96). Olivares took the same line. Both were much more concerned about each other. As their mutual relations deteriorated to the point of war in 1635, they retained a common concern that Charles should not tie himself decisively to the other. He was to be kept interested, but left dangling (**160**).

There was no doubt where Charles's own preferences lay. He never really trusted the French, and further provocative remarks by French ministers and sea captains about the sovereignty of the seas confirmed his doubts. He was prepared to negotiate at length with them, but always as a second best, and in part with the intention of putting diplomatic pressure on Spain. Any Anglo-French initiative on behalf of the Palatinate would require the deployment of armies, and the assistance of a range of Protestant allies. It would be costly, complicated and, even if some or all the Palatinate was taken, held out no guarantee that it would be returned to Elizabeth and her family. The Spanish seemed to Charles more dependable. He had been impressed during his visit to Madrid in 1623 by the dignified way in which they conducted business and by the deep respect which they evidently had for established authority. They also offered the possibility of a diplomatic solution. They still had in their possession much of the Lower Palatinate, which their forces had helped to take in the early 1620s, while their imperial cousins continued to exercise control over the Upper Palatinate, currently occupied by Maximilian of Bavaria. In addition, Spain was aware of the vulnerability of its supply lines to the Spanish Netherlands, and might welcome English maritime assistance in curbing the aggression of the Dutch. Charles, who had his own reasons for wishing to restore the reputation of the English Navy, saw no reason why he should not take steps towards the recovery of the Palatinate while asserting his right to be sovereign of the Narrow, or British, Seas.

Where Elizabeth Tudor and his father had touched only lightly on the matter of sovereignty of the seas, recognising that force of arms resolved the matter sooner or later, Charles from the start of his reign was insistent on what he saw as his right to it in British waters (**167**). Despite the failure of his fleets during the 1620s, he struck his first medal asserting his maritime dominion in 1630.

Much of his keenest attention, in the early days of the personal rule, was given to the Navy (**166**). After an exhaustive tour of the dockyards, he took up again, at John Coke's suggestion, the shipbuilding programme Buckingham's commission had followed between 1619 and 1624. By 1634 four new men-of-war had been built and declared seaworthy, the plans made and the keel laid at Woolwich for his new great ship, the remarkable *Sovereign of the Seas*, and one or two much-needed smaller craft added to the strength (**34, 207**). While Sir John Borough scoured the records in the Tower for his treatise affirming Charles's sovereignty of the British seas, ready by March 1634, and John Selden prepared his *Mare Clausum* for publication, the Admiralty drew up a new set of rules of behaviour within those waters; and Charles in April appointed a new and exclusive Council committee for foreign affairs, the first since Buckingham's death. He was intent on launching a major fleet, reflecting the new strength of the Royal Navy and capable of enforcing his rules, before the autumn (**167**). It was to contain appreciably more of the King's own ships – as distinct from armed merchantmen – than any of the expeditions of the 1620s (**47**). Charles had hopes of securing funding from Spain; but despite drawn-out talks, based on the secret treaty of 1631, it gradually became clear that Spain had not got the funds to spare even for a loan, and Charles had, too late for his immediate purposes, to turn with Weston and the Council to consider, with such help as the dying Noy could give, some form of ship money (**127**). The Tower records were once more searched for precedents and, although none quite fitted, a scheme was rapidly devised. But as a consequence, the fleet was not able to put to sea by the autumn of 1634; and Charles, to his chagrin, lost the chance of earning himself 'an infinite reputation' by 'making the proudest of... [his] neighbours look about them' (**167**, pp. 176–7).

By the time the fleet did get to sea, in May 1635, France and Spain were formally at war; and the Emperor was in the process of settling a war-weary Germany while strengthening his ties with the elderly but ever-ambitious Maximilian of Bavaria by assuring him, under the terms of the Treaty of Prague, of his continued possession of the Upper Palatinate (**162**). The death at the battle of Lützen in November 1632 of Gustavus Adolphus, whose triumphant progress had always lifted up the godly in England, closely followed by that of the exiled, and in imperial eyes outlawed, Frederick V, had done nothing to help the Palatine cause in Germany [**doc. 20**] (also **41**). After the Emperor's forces had resoundingly, if rather fortuitously, beaten the Swedes at Nördlingen in September 1634, wiping out most of their advances in recent years, the princes of Germany, and especially John George of Saxony, were ready for compromise. All but Bernard of Saxe-Weimar of the more important were prepared to accept the Emperor's offer to abandon the principle of the 1629 Edict of Restitution, which had sought to remove Protestant domination in north Germany, and to restore lands to their holders in 1627 for a forty-year period during which their final settlement could be arranged (**162**). In order to hasten the peace along, they agreed to exclude Frederick's heir, Charles Louis, from the amnesty. The dynastic interests of one family were no longer to prolong the war for all, and must form the subject of a separate settlement with the Emperor. In July, Ferdinand encouraged the widowed Maximilian to sign the Peace by offering one of his daughters in marriage and by confirming him in his electorate, formerly Frederick's. In little over a year, Maximilian had the male heir he had long wanted. While Frederick lived, he had been determined to negotiate for the return of the entire Palatinate and his electoral title; since his death, however, and despite the doubts of Elizabeth, Charles had more scope for flexibility. His problem in 1635 was that his options were rapidly closing in. Much had changed in the year since his fleet had first hoped to show off its new strength.

Charles's immediate aim, nevertheless, was to assert his naval sovereignty over the French, and Lindsey, his first ship-money admiral, was soon in trouble for not actively seeking confrontations with Louis's navy (**167**). Richelieu, then and subsequently, made sure that it kept a low profile in Channel waters. However, Charles's fleet undoubtedly had a presence (**47**). Its twenty or more heavily armed men-of-war commanded respect from all but intrepid privateers who continued to operate behind its back, and from some English merchant captains, disgruntled at the attention being paid to their movements. Gradually, too, much-needed faster and lighter vessels were added (**207**). Operating from its base in the Downs, off Dover, the fleet not only swept Channel waters, but at times reached north through the herring fishing grounds to Buchan Ness, and south into the Bay of Biscay. The Dutch treated it courteously; and its ships, often engaged on convoy work, alone in Europe had access to all continental ports. In northern waters, there was some shift in trading advantage to England despite continuing piracy, and Dover, for the moment, became a flourishing entrepot (**131**, **132**, **200**, **125**). Each year's fleet was crewed by about 3,000 sailors; and although the sons of the gentry were not on the whole disposed to join in the King's service and it never became the rallying point that Noy and others hoped it might be, the Navy which defected to Parliament in 1642 was altogether superior to the fleets of the 1620s in organisation and firepower (**47**). And in the richly decorated, 1,500-ton *Sovereign of the Seas*, launched prematurely at Charles's insistence in the autumn of 1637, it possessed the first genuine three-decker, closer in tonnage, length, armaments and sail configuration to the ships of the line of Nelson's day than to the men-of-war of Drake's (**87, 34**). It was Charles's misfortune that the great gilded ship, richly embellished with the symbols of England's maritime past, should have begun its sea trials at a moment when his foreign policy had run aground [**doc. 27**].

Despite his lack of financial support, Charles had based his strategy for the recovery of the Palatinate on cooperation with Spain. Commercial traffic between the two nations had continued all through the war of 1625–30, as it had in the 1580s and 1590s; and in 1631 Cottington had also played a part in concluding a commercial agreement with the Genoese bankers, who funded the government of the Spanish Netherlands, by which New World bullion would be carried to Dunkirk in English ships (**105, 200**). The King's own men-of-war at times took consignments, at least twice evading the full effects of the duties exacted at Dover, possibly with political intent. But more generally, the peace-keeping role which the ship-money fleet adopted was of more benefit to Spain than to any of its neighbours, for it reduced the chances of Dutch aggression, and encouraged Olivares to send several large armadas northwards, with provisions and raw levies, returning with skilled Walloon soldiers needed for service against the French. At times, the sight of the tall masts of Spanish galleons, hugging the English coastline as they stole up-Channel, awakened memories of '88. At others, as the Dutch sharpened their watch, Spanish troops had to be landed at Plymouth and marched to Dover, so that they could be safely 'wafted' over to Dunkirk. But, until the autumn of 1639, Spanish casualties were few.

Yet for all the maritime cooperation with Spain, Charles's hopes were misplaced. There was little chance of regaining any part of the Palatinate through the good offices of either branch of the Habsburgs. Spain professed no long-term interest in the Lower Palatinate, even though its possession brought it closer to the centre of European affairs; but Spain was not going to relinquish its interest in its 'bridge on the Rhine' as Philip IV called it, until it had obtained from the Emperor a commitment to help Spain crush the Dutch, as it had been urging for many years. Ferdinand, however, preferred to keep a wary eye on Sweden, and had no wish to upset Maximilian by readily sanctioning the ceding of any part of the Palatinate. Frail now, he knew Maximilian's vote would soon be needed to ensure the succession of his son Ferdinand as emperor. Spain and the Empire had developed divergent outlooks. In retrospect, the taking of the Palatinate had been the last example of concerted action on a large scale by the two branches of the Habsburgs; during the 1620s they had begun to grow apart. The Austrians had preoccupations in central Europe; the Spanish, although tied to Flanders, looked westwards for their economic survival. Although Charles's hopes largely depended on Spanish intervention, there were no persuasive grounds for supposing the Spaniards could exert any compelling influence on their imperial cousins, whom they were already irritating by their attempts to control, through the cardinal-infant at Brussels, the ways in which their subsidies were used.

The ratification of the Peace of Prague, at the Diet at Ratisbon late in the summer of 1636, made plain the inconsequence of Charles's main strategy. Apparently buoyed up by the naive optimism of the newly arrived English agent at Vienna, John Taylor, Charles sent Arundel on a hurried but dignified embassy to the Emperor, in the hope of settling the Palatinate issue once and for all in the wake of the Prague agreements (**196**). Arundel's formal instructions set stiff terms; but, as his old friend Elizabeth sadly discovered, he had privately been told to be flexible. Arundel's haughty bearing may not have encouraged deep consideration of possible long-term solutions; but for the moment there were few practical courses to pursue. He and his company derived what benefit they could from the cultural opportunities their journey offered, while noting on all sides the devastation of war (**196**). Politically it was, as the Earl had supposed it would be, a 'desperate...business' (**44**, vol. 2, p. 3).

As the expected news of Arundel's failure filtered back to Court, the francophiles there made another effort to push Charles's foreign policy in a parliamentary direction [**doc. 25**]. One of the first duties of the 1635 ship-money fleet had been to carry Laud's friend Viscount Scudamore across the Channel on his appointment as ambassador to France; and at the same time as Arundel left in haste for the Imperial Court, Robert Sydney, Earl of Leicester, made a more leisured progress to Paris to lend incisive reinforcement to the hidebound Scudamore (**8**). Negotiations along familiar lines had thus been taking place for many months. By early 1636, John Coke reckoned that sixteen inconclusive sets of propositions and responses had already passed between the two courts. Sufficient progress had been made to arouse strong suspicions at Court and within the Council during the summer that the hispanophiles Cottington and Windebank had encouraged Walter Stewart, a well-connected captain of one of the King's men-of-war, to flout the strict regulations for transporting silver to Flanders by neglecting to land two-thirds of the bullion at Dover in return for bills of exchange provided by Charles. Stewart profited handsomely as a result; but Cottington and Windebank's probable aim was to sow doubts in Louis XIII's mind about the strength of Charles's commitment as the Anglo-French agreement neared completion (**5**). At the end of 1636, with Arundel for the first time set against the Habsburg interest and Warwick and others at Court pressing the case for a more Protestant approach to the Palatine problem, Charles toyed with the idea of sending out Frederick's young heir Charles Louis, then at Court as a living reminder of his mother's plight, to strafe Spanish shipping (**6**). But while Charles would supply the ships, his nephew was to fly his own standard so as not to suggest to Spain that England was once more at war with her. However, lack of firm financial support from his Protestant allies, and perhaps evidence of puritanical enthusiasm at home for what looked like a move at last towards a blue-water strategy, caused Charles's interest to cool rapidly. It was at this point, in February 1637, when he had no defined foreign policy and was under pressure to summon Parliament in preparation for joint action with France and his Protestant allies, that Charles sought the judges' opinion about his right to levy ship money. He was in effect seeking to establish the freedom to determine his own foreign policy, whatever it might be.

At much the same time, and to the incredulity of Elizabeth and her correspondent Laud, Charles determined to resume his unsuccessful attempt to impose licences for fishing in the North Sea, as part of his claim to sovereignty, on the Dutch herring fleets (**5**). The Dutch had supposed that the need for Protestant allies might have dissuaded him, especially after his concern for sovereignty of the Narrow Seas had ruffled the French during their recent dealings. Exploitation of the North Sea fishing grounds might have helped the English economy; but as one of the London aldermen, Sir

Henry Garway, once told Laud at the Council table, the English, unlike the Dutch, were not dedicated eaters of fish; and there was little commercial enthusiasm for Charles's attempts to establish royal fishing societies in either England or Scotland (**5**, 15 June 1637). The Dutch fleets were unrivalled in size; but in 1636 the King's ships had managed to raise only £502 from sales of licences, a good deal less than from convoying duties (**125, 167**). In 1637, Charles again signed hundreds of blanks in readiness and had them packed in the familiar black box; but he decided not to risk further humiliation to his own ships, and entrusted the operation to one of the merchantmen sailing with them. So limited was its captain's success, however, that he and other mariners were afterwards sworn by the Council to silence, while the sovereign of the seas gave the matter further thought (**19, 167**).

That same summer, the ship-money fleet had very little to do, as its admiral Northumberland bitterly complained to his confidant, Wentworth [**doc. 27**]. It had put to sea in untidy fashion, as its captains drifted back after the collapse of Charles Louis's proposed venture, which a number of them – including Northumberland – would have preferred to be on (**6**). A small detachment under Rainsborough had sailed at last to Sallee against 'Turkish' pirates, a persistent nuisance never properly addressed by Charles, suggesting that protecting shipping was never intended to be a prime purpose of the ship-money fleets, whatever might be said in the King's name (**47**). One of Northumberland's few duties was to return Charles Louis and his brother Rupert to the Continent, an indication of their mother's reading of Charles's mind. He had never moved far from his preference for Spain; and even in circumstances of minimal hope, he set up in May 1637 a new Council committee, with Laud, Arundel and Cottington among its members, to treat with the latest Spanish ambassador, Oñate, whom Walter Stewart had brought to Dover. Oñate himself thought it of no consequence (**99**).

The Scottish troubles gave Charles a new sense of purpose and direction, and were welcomed by both Richelieu and Olivares as a means of deflecting him from other undertakings. It was while part of the 1639 fleet was away in the north that the Dutch for a month trapped the biggest of the Spanish armadas in the Downs, the English fleet's own base. Charles sold food and powder to the Spaniards, and sought to negotiate protection money with Madrid, while English courtiers had a grandstand view of proceedings (**167**). But in the end, the Dutch sent in their fireships, scattered the main Spanish fleet, and dealt a major blow to Charles's pride. Worse was to follow, when the bulk of the Navy which he had carefully nurtured through the 1630s defected in 1642 to the parliamentary side, where it came under the command of the Earl of Warwick (**47**). It had never, as Maximilian of Bavaria once dismissively remarked to the Emperor, had a clear-cut role in relation to the Palatinate (**196**). It did not carry soldiers, it lacked parliamentary backing, and it had no obvious point from which to attack the Empire. Instead, it was obliged to spend much of its time on formalities, exacting the deference claimed by its royal master. When, by the Treaty of Westphalia in 1648, Charles Louis eventually recovered the Lower Palatinate, and was given a new electoral title, it was through the good offices of France and Sweden.

# 10  Religion

## The peace of the Church

By 1629 Charles was as anxious to quieten the Church as he was to rid himself of Parliament. Doctrinal differences had taken on a new edge. How serious they were is a matter for debate. Peter White has argued strongly for the underlying unity of the broad-based English Church, and contends that these tensions were little more than a short-term response to the wars against Spain, especially, and France, for the moment heightening the exchanges between the more zealous Calvinists and those anti-Calvinists whom they supposed to be tainted with popery (**217**). Even as peace approached, however, Charles felt he had to insist on the peace and quiet of the Church; and others, notably Nicholas Tyacke and Peter Lake, have emphasised both the depth and the longevity of its internal differences, as well as the degree of change which accompanied the accession of Charles I (**213, 137**). James had always been guarded about his own religious position; but although in his later years he took more account of anti-Calvinist views, the clergy chosen to represent him at the international conference at Dort in 1618–19 all came from the mainstream of English Protestant thought (**137**). The English delegation had consisted entirely of moderate and responsible Calvinist clergy, ranged firmly against the Dutch remonstrants (as the followers of Arminius were known); and the anti-Calvinist clergy had all stayed at home (**213**).

The Dort delegation, although all predestinarians, had however differed among themselves about the detailed nature of their beliefs. The majority were traditional supralapsarians*, holding with Whitgift, Abbot and the unratified Lambeth articles of 1595 that, even before the Fall, God had chosen a limited number of human beings for election to eternal salvation, while the rest were damned as reprobates (**137**). The Cambridge theologians Samuel Ward and John Davenant, in a slightly more liberal variation, argued then and subsequently that Christ had died for all mankind, but that man's depravity since the Fall had meant that only the Elect could benefit from his sacrifice. Ward and Davenant were 'hypothetical universalists', believers in a once-universal salvation, and to that extent closer to the anti-Calvinist belief in an enduring universal grace; but they were still emphatically Calvinist (**213**). They had joined in Bishop Carleton's riposte to *Appello Caesarem* in 1626 which sought to rebut Montagu's claim that there was a gap between the true meaning of the Thirty-nine Articles and the Calvinists' 'puritanical' gloss on them. Nevertheless, although Charles eventually ordered Montagu's writings to be burned, it was not before the latter's polemics had been officially declared consonant with the doctrines of the Church of England, and he was about to become a bishop. There can be no doubt that Montagu had seized his political moment; and there was equally no doubt that leading Calvinist clergy recognised the need, at the start of the personal rule, to make afresh the case for the old orthodoxy. For at Court the balance of favour had shifted perceptibly away from them [**doc. 16**].

It was by no means clear how far Charles was prepared, after his Declaration on the Articles of Religion in 1628, to allow discussion of central religious issues; and Davenant may have set out in 1629–30 to establish what the limits were (**137**) [**doc. 16**]. James had made Davenant Bishop of Salisbury back in 1621, but he was one of those soundly Calvinist bishops who advanced no further under Charles. In 1629, however, he had given a Lenten sermon at Court on the first part of Romans 6: 23 – 'the wages of sin is death' – and in 1630 he returned to give a second on the remainder of that verse: 'The gift of God is eternal life, through Jesus Christ our Lord', which he related to the seventeenth of the Thirty-nine Articles, which deals specifically with predestination. Charles was present at the sermon, and afterwards had Davenant summoned before the Privy Council. There he was harangued at some length by the Archbishop of York, Harsnet, now a Privy Councillor, and although he defended himself by pointing out that he had said nothing that was contrary to Article XVII or any other Article, he was told to avoid such subjects in future as it was 'the King's will... that for the peace of the Church these high questions should be forborne'. Next day, when he went to kiss the King's hand, Charles confirmed that 'he would not have this high point meddled with or debated one way or [the] other... it was too high for the people's understanding, and the points which concern reformation and newness of life were more needful and profitable' (**98**, p. 309). There was to be no scope for latitude. No Calvinist preacher was heard at Paul's Cross after 1628 (**213**). Yet the anti-Calvinist message continued to be delivered, and so at times were doctrines distinctly Roman in character, as happened in the University of Cambridge where there was a clear divide in religious sentiment (**119**).

## Rival myths

Such lapses scarcely helped towards the peace and quiet of the Church. For one of the two countervailing myths which were current in early Stuart England was that of a popish conspiracy, which subsumed Protestant fears of what the Roman Catholic Church and its defenders seemed to stand for. The threats to national security posed by the Spanish Armada in 1588, the Gunpowder Plot, and the various invasion scares of the 1620s remained fresh in the memory, as did the rejoicing over Prince Charles's escape from the clutches of Spain in 1623. Parliamentary debates about, and lists of, popish officeholders had helped to keep up tension during the war years. A well-developed thread of suspicion ran deep in the English consciousness, no matter whether England was at peace or at war. As Peter Lake has shown, thoroughgoing Calvinism may be defined in terms of its opposition to popery, its rejection of a seemingly superstitious but mechanistic approach to religion which appeared to condone idolatry on the one hand and to urge justification by works* on the other (**136**). Anti-Calvinism (or Arminianism) in England looked to Calvinists to be disturbingly popish (**110**). Its emphasis on the sacramental elements in religion elevated the role of the clergy, now described as priests not ministers, and seemed to endanger the local ascendancy of the gentry as patrons of the Church. The diminishing importance of the pulpit, and the restrictions on preaching the Word, threatened to leave the mass of the people in spiritual ignorance, especially of the possibilities for the non-elect of receiving God's blessing [doc. 18] (**136, 60**). As the Book of Common Prayer seemed to be taking precedence over the Bible, godly parish clergy grew increasingly anxious about catechising their flocks, and popular printers began to respond to the need for appropriate reading (**85**).

The Catholics themselves comprised only about 1 per cent of the population, but they had sufficient traditional areas of strength to sustain doubts about their purposes. In Northamptonshire and

Sussex, for example, they endured a fractious relationship with their Protestant neighbours (**94**). They also caused concern by their concentration to the west of the City of London and at Court itself, where the papal representative in the later 1630s, George Con, achieved some notable conversions, if little else. Charles hardly helped matters by his continual, if almost unavoidable, cultural contacts with courts and artists who happened to be popish (**86, 109**).

Against the fears of a popish conspiracy, the Arminians set a counter myth: that since the 1580s, radical Calvinist gentry and clergy had made common cause with excitable and irresponsible popular spirits in order to undermine the government of both Church and state (**136**). This was an assertion repeatedly made by Laud in sermons during the 1620s, especially in that preached at the opening of the 1626 Parliament, and it supplied a variation on the theme which Laud and Heath elaborated in the draft documents they prepared for the King during the same period (**31, 79**) [**doc. 9**]. Charles thus had strong political grounds for wanting religious peace, and had made it clear that he thought he stood the best chance of receiving it through the Arminian clergy who, in the later 1620s, began to dominate the management of the Church. Attacks in print and pulpit on Laud and his fellow bishops, or on other aspects of government or courtly behaviour, were interpreted as seditious and were harshly punished in Star Chamber. Laud almost invariably recommended the severest sentence, as Leighton (1630), Prynne (1634 and 1637) and Burton and Bastwick (both 1637) were to find out. Prynne, for example, was twice sentenced to life imprisonment and the loss of his ears, not wholly removed on the first occasion, and fined £5,000; in 1634 he was also stripped of his Oxford degree and expelled from Lincoln's Inn, where he had read for the bar. Yet he was no dangerous radical. His dislike of present dispositions at Court sprang from a powerful longing for past values; but he was treated instead as an innovator and incendiary, seeking to undermine state and Church (**143**). Burton, Bastwick and Prynne were all professional men, between them representing the gospel, medicine and the law. Yet, sensitive though Charles usually was to social gradations, their status was not enough to save them. Zealous but peaceable Calvinist gentry like Sir Simonds D'Ewes were severely shaken at the lack of respect they were shown [**doc. 22**]. As victims, however, they acquired a new status as popular heroes, attracting support far exceeding that of the readership of their published work.

## The Church in the localities

How far anti-Calvinism took hold on the Church in the countryside is hard to determine, and for an answer we must await detailed local studies. Historically, its strength had rested in certain university colleges and at Court. How clearly its message was understood in the localities, and how many clergy were preaching that message with conviction, is at present open to question. Like extremer Calvinism, it was almost certainly a minority interest, although a vociferous one. Somewhere between the two rested the majority of the English laity, less deeply engaged and usually unheard before 1641 (**157**). At least twenty-five clergy from the City of London and nine English counties are known to have provoked accusations of Arminianism, and others were very probably harassed on less specific grounds (**213**). But clergy tend to live long lives, and livings only slowly to fall vacant; so the spread of Arminian support may well have depended as much on established clergy declaring themselves as on new blood coming in.

Indeed, reduced to particular persons and places, the clash of two ideologies sometimes becomes hard to discern, although the untidiness in the working out must not be taken as indicating that Laud and his royal master were not bent on establishing conformity to a new orthodoxy. That they were may itself have helped to promote apparent inconsistency (**156, 213**). Thus Samuel Hoard, who wrote either alone or jointly a number of cogent Arminian tracts during the 1630s and engaged with Bishop Davenant as early as 1633, was the puritan Earl of Warwick's former household chaplain, and had been appointed by him in 1625 to one of his best livings, at Moreton in Essex. He was to remain there, undisturbed, until his death just before the Restoration, despite the county's reputation for radical Calvinism. Hoard was a convert to Arminianism at some time after 1629 (**98**). Where once he had believed, with Article XVII, in 'the unspeakable comfort to godly persons' of election, he had, as he confessed in *God's Love to Mankind* (1633, p. 91), come to consider instead that it 'cutteth the very sinews of religion and pulleth away the strongest inducements to a holy life' by breeding spiritual complacency, a matter of continual concern to parish clergy. John Gore, another Arminian preacher and writer during the 1630s, lived only a few miles from Hoard, and he too may have been a recent convert, for his patron, Sir John Mead, was part of a multi-branched but often strongly Calvinist family (of whom the best known was Joseph, the broad-minded and ever curious Fellow of Christ's, Cambridge) and had himself married into the Corbetts of Norfolk. His brother-in-law, Sir John Corbett, had allegedly been put out of the commission of peace after a local popish conspiracy, before dying young in 1628 after his experiences as one of the five knights denied bail as a Loan refuser; and John's brother Miles was to be one of the regicides. Mead may never have been as firmly Calvinist as Warwick; but in his own way he also followed events at Court, and like the Earl he may well have recognised the potential value of a supposedly right-thinking and notably articulate incumbent. Certainly, when Warwick was anxious to protect the lecturer Thomas Hooker from Laud, he used one of his more moderate and responsible Calvinist parish clergy, Sam Collins of Braintree, as an effective intermediary (**5**) [also **doc. 18**]. Similarly, William Lord Maynard, who had Arminian leanings, intervened with Laud in 1631 on behalf of Hooker's ally Thomas Weld, doubtless on the promptings of his own Calvinist wife (**38**).

In the special case of the palatine county of Durham, where the Bishop headed its administration, Neile between 1617 and 1628 showed himself able to work in sensible cooperation with the Calvinist gentry, and to avoid continual friction with either cathedral or parochial clergy, while pushing ahead with innovation. On his departure, the intemperate Peter Smart, one of the prebendaries, took the opportunity to attack recent Arminian innovations. Yet he received only muted support within the county, even though his views were those of a Calvinist conservative, and were embraced by the Commons in their attacks on Arminian clergy in high places in 1628–29 (**208**). From 1632, Neile once more exercised oversight over Durham as Archbishop of York; but although he kept a close watch on its Calvinist bishop, Morton, he may well have pressed less hard because he knew the foundations had been well laid. Elsewhere in the province he left no doubt that he was still firmly wedded to the ideals of the old Durham House set (**97, 80** and Foster in **82**).

The majority of the English may well have preferred the comfortable rhythms of the Prayer Book to the technicalities of predestination* (**157**). Certainly, neither Charles nor Laud was much concerned about doctrinal niceties. The King wanted the Church's affairs to be put in order, so that it could properly play its role as an adjunct of his kingship, as the Navy did in the British seas and the gentry were supposed to do on their country estates. Many of the details of how that order was to be achieved were left to Laud, as in the case of the new statutes for the University of Oxford, and the character of much of Church policy during the 1630s inescapably reflects his personality (**188**). In many respects Charles and Laud worked closely together, and responsibility for individual measures is often hard to determine. Laud habitually invoked the King's name in his own directions to the clergy, doubtless after putting ideas into his head; but he was no confidant of the King, who had chosen to promote him for his own reasons and who in due course was to cast him aside. Church policy in the 1630s had two basic aims: one was to restore the economic fortunes of the clergy, and the other was to secure a broad measure of conformity to their chosen standards in doctrine and worship, which included encouragement in decoration of churches and the introduction of images which went far beyond the narrow limits allowed by Whitgift and other earlier Church leaders, for whom the Word was always paramount (**52**).

Feeble management of resources had left some post-Reformation clergy at all levels inadequately provided for (**111**). To venture at recovery was not an Arminian novelty. Some Jacobean Calvinists, like Bishop Bridgeman of Chester, had for many years struggled to recover the assets of an under-endowed diocese which predecessors had let slip away into lay hands; and in his case his efforts had given him a grasping reputation which did not help him during his rough handling by Charles in 1633 (**168**). But set as they now were within the generally authoritarian context of much of Charles's government, such attempts were calculated to unsettle the gentry more than ever. In 1629 the bishops were sent to reside in their dioceses, and by instructions then and in 1634, were ordered to husband their resources and arrange their leases in a businesslike way. Laud condemned the practice of agreeing leases for three lives, and tried to insist that none should be longer than twenty-one years (**108**). That worked well enough in the diocese of Canterbury; but elsewhere bishops, including Neile, recognised the social value of the longer lease, which helped to tie the senior gentry to them. This consideration had apparently been lost on Laud who, as Archbishop of Canterbury from August 1633, did not even share his predecessor's liking for entertaining the Kent gentry at Lambeth (**107**). The practice had made Abbot popular, but to Laud it looked too much like an attempt to buy support – a view which was worthy, but uncourtly and unworldly. Neile and others continued to lease for lives where appropriate.

But if Laud was distant from most of the laity, he was, as

Prynne found, overtly hostile to the common lawyers, especially to the judges at their head. The reissue of James's Book of Sports* in 1633 was provoked by the judges on the Western circuit rashly siding with the puritan gentry of Somerset in wishing to preserve their restrictive views of the Sabbath; and the unexpected dismissal of Chief Justice Heath in September 1634 owed much to his rigorous – and in Laud's eyes, inflexible – handling of disputes over actual or claimed Church properties which came before him in Common Pleas (**16, 59, 135**). His pliable successor, Finch, before appointment promised Laud a different approach, as in the disciplinary sphere did the equally malleable Sir John Lambe, who in rather dubious circumstances replaced the outstanding civilian* of his day, Sir Henry Marten, as Dean of the Arches soon after Abbot's death. The recovery of Church estates through the common law courts was however a slow and piecemeal business, more likely to provoke disquiet among the gentry than effect any early improvement in the economic condition of the Church. It had none of the immediate impact of Charles's revocation in Scotland. Yet much of Laud's voluminous and seemingly all-embracing correspondence is taken up with the subject as well as with abuse of common lawyers, in Ireland as in England (**212**). Because of it, he established a cordial relationship with Bishop Bridgeman in the later 1630s, appreciating him, for all his Calvinist tendencies, distinctly more than his own primate Neile evidently did.

## The visitations

Laud wasted little time after his preferment in 1628 to the see of London in trying to put his own house in order. He visited the whole diocese in person in 1631, winning reluctant puritan approval for his ridiculing of clergy whose dress was too resplendent for his own simple tastes; but he found the Essex lecturers* impudent and elusive [**doc. 19**]. Most had only recently come to the county, as though drawing closer to Warwick in stormy times, and were soon on the move again. Although the wave of migration to the New World in the 1630s was by no means entirely for spiritual reasons, zealous ministers and their flocks constituted a regular element. Laud was more successful in meeting those in the City of London, however, for it abounded in lectureships. Many of them served individual parishes instead of whole towns as was usual elsewhere, and were filled at local expense by learned and vigorous preachers supplying needs the Church was otherwise slow to meet. They provided an alternative voice to the parish clergy and thus were always likely to be more radically Calvinist. When Laud became Bishop of London there were an estimated 121 lecturers* in the City, of whom fifty-nine were puritan. By 1633, he had reduced the overall number to eighty-eight; yet no fewer than forty-six of the survivors were puritan, and those forty-six preached approximately sixty sermons a week in an urban area of one square mile. Indeed, throughout the 1630s, the proportion of puritan lecturers* was always more than half, slightly more than it had been in 1628 (**183**). But, also in 1633, Laud succeeded in putting an end to the work of the feoffees for impropriations after the court of Exchequer condemned them for setting themselves up as a body holding property without the sanction of the King. This group of solid and responsible London merchants, clergy and lawyers had, as committed Calvinists, raised over £6,000 since 1625 to buy more than thirty church livings, and to augment the stipends of numerous lecturers* and other clergy (**111**). They had done so in order to extend godliness into the darker corners of the land; and in each of those thirty parishes they, as patrons, almost certainly had more influence than the local bishop on the kind of sermons and Church services their clergy provided.

As in the country parishes, Laud had not pressed the London lecturers* on finer points of doctrine, but had sought conformity in dress and ceremonial; and many gave formal acceptance to such terms. He well knew the shallowness of this conformity; and later, as Primate, received further criticism of his criterion from his vicar-general, Archbishop Abbot's kinsman Sir Nathaniel Brent. Of the serpentine Stephen Marshall, a future preacher to the Long Parliament, Brent observed: 'No man doubteth but he hath an inconformable heart; but externally he observeth all' (**5**, March 1637). But to Laud the surplice and vestments had a deeper significance; with ritual, on which he was also insistent, they were essential elements in the expression of anti-Calvinist worship within, and central management of, the Church. He knew that, away from the eye of authority, zealous Calvinist clergy might soon lapse again. As a visitor to Lancashire – in Neile's province – told him in 1637: there 'all the orders of the Church go down the wind' and in Preston and Manchester 'they call the surplices the rags of Rome... and will suffer no organs nor... sign of the cross' (**5**, 25 April 1637).

As Archbishop of Canterbury, Laud began at once to prepare for the first metropolitical visitation of the southern province since the reign of Henry VIII. Neile undertook a similar exercise in the province of York. Laud's preliminary instructions to Brent in February 1634 ordered him to scrutinise the statutes by which each cathedral governed itself; listed clergy – very few overall – known to be careless about dress or ceremonials; specified those other local problems so far known to need attention; and strictly warned him and his assistants not to treat the communion table with the undue familiarity they had done in the past (**5**). The visitation articles themselves provided the fullest expression of Arminian concern for dress, ceremonial, the material assets of incumbents and the fabric of the churches which the southern province had ever had; and their detail consorted ill with the restless pace with which Brent conducted affairs (**31**). Although the whole process of visiting the southern province extended over three years, beginning with Laud's old enemy John Williams' diocese of Lincoln in 1634 and ending in 1637 with London and the Welsh sees, it took at best a brief view of current circumstances, leaving business unstarted as well as unfinished. In the diocese of London it probably made less impact than Laud had done in 1631, as he had feared it would; he had only been dissuaded from undertaking it himself by the weight of precedent against him (**31**).

Much was left to the archdeacons' and commissaries' courts, accustomed as they were to dealing many times a year with all forms of spiritual and moral shortcomings. Neither they nor the bishop, who visited every third year, made much contact in these respects with the gentry who, as patrons of more than half the Church's livings, often exercised a controlling interest in local religious practices (**111**). The Church's leaders could antagonise by their policies; but they were rarely in a position to achieve their ends without the goodwill of gentry and town authorities (**120**). Much, though, was to depend on circumstances in individual dioceses. In Chichester, for example, the clergy greeted Brent with deference rather than enthusiasm, while the gentry were indifferent until the issue of altar rails brought them into open conflict with the bishop's Arminian supporters. However, in both Buckingham-shire (part of the huge diocese of Lincoln, where Williams remained contrary) and Nottinghamshire (in the diocese of York) there were signs of cooperation over both church buildings and discipline (**95, 151**). In Norwich, Bishop Wren took the lecturers* on; but so provocative did he prove to the godly that his gesture in sparing a few of the lecturers* was almost lost from sight. Few bishops were less popular, and *Newes from Ipswich*, the pamphlet for which

Prynne, who may have been its author, was tried in Star Chamber in 1637, made the most of it (**133, 142**).

At Colchester (in the diocese of London), where Bastwick had his family and in which Burton and Prynne also took an interest, the full import of Laud's innovations was widely understood; but it was still possible to mock the detail of his programme (**81, 141**). One parish eventually erected its altar rails, but then provided 'divers forms' so that parishioners could receive the sacraments sitting down. In another, a churchwarden paid for the new rails from his own pocket, and then found the leader of the resistance to his altar-rail rate elected as his successor. Some rails were erected just in time to be torn down by well-directed, if drunken, levies waiting to be sent north for service against the covenanting Scots in 1640, who, despite their condition, also managed to locate the homes of leading papists. The two myths, one Calvinist and the other Arminian, were about to collide.

Either from ignorance or a well-developed reticence, the bishops kept much hidden from higher authority and the King's dogged oversight. Not all managed to report annually; and when they did, their accounts, as summarised by the two Primates, were sometimes as painfully short of solid information as were those of any petty constable to quarter sessions* (**28**). In London in 1635, Bishop Juxon had to rely on his own circumscribed knowledge after three of his four archdeacons had made no return at all to him (**31**). Neile had a similar problem in the north, and never seems to have had much confidence in his bishops at Chester and Carlisle, both Calvinists, or in the accuracy of their affirmations [**doc. 21**]. While the reform programme of the 1630s undoubtedly received a warm welcome in some quarters, the political overtones which it carried were sufficient to ensure its overall failure [**doc. 29**].

For too many of the Calvinist gentry, Charles's religious policy had pressed innovation in the name of orthodoxy, and had sought, unsuccessfully, to prevent free discussion in the cause of peace and quiet (**122**). It had altered the criteria by which, through established forms of worship, they expressed their loyalty to the Crown; and it had, inadvertently, helped to confirm fears that Charles's government had palpable leanings towards popery. Such were their apprehensions that they never appreciated that little Laud, the main focus of Calvinist hostility, in practice had no more love for Rome than they did.

# Part Four: Assessment

## 11 The Trouble with Charles I

Charles's problems were never entirely of his own making. His inheritance in 1625 was undoubtedly a secure one; but there were also weaknesses within the Jacobean polity. The monarchy was already clearly under-funded in peacetime by 1603, and it was to remain so in circumstances which made the Exchequer judgement on impositions in Bate's case, as interpreted by the Crown, both financially rewarding and politically contentious. The union of the crowns of England and Scotland had not led on to a wider union of the kingdoms, leaving the Scots imperfectly integrated into the new arrangement. As with the fragile unity of the Church of England, much depended on the person of the King. The flight of Frederick V and his wife Elizabeth from Bohemia and the fall of the Palatinate to Habsburg forces had exposed the limitations of Jacobean foreign policy. It might have paid more heed to France; for, as Charles discovered during his stay in Madrid in 1623, his father exercised no compelling influence on Spain.

Charles's mission had nevertheless been a foolhardy one; and the cheering which greeted his return home with Buckingham that October was prompted by relief rather than admiration. Even so, he never seems to have received such an expression of public warmth again. He did little to prompt one. He had a less comfortable relationship with his subjects than James, and entirely lacked the deft assurance of Elizabeth. His Court gave strong expression to the formal attributes of kingship; but he rarely came into contact with large gatherings of his subjects. Few of them ever saw him. For his fellow Scots, he was a distant, and in many ways foreign, king with little appreciation of Scottish ways. The Irish for their part had little expectation that he would ever visit them, although Wentworth set about building a palace in County Kildare on the off-chance. Even the English found Charles remote and unbending, as well as difficult to deal with. He had a keen appreciation of privacy, and was always sparing in his public appearances, even in circumstances in which they might have been expected.

Charles had a deep-seated suspicion, bordering on paranoia, of popular sentiment and the popular voice (**79**). To him, they were synonymous with disorder, and even disloyalty. Those MPs who criticised his administration tended to be regarded not as candid friends but as opponents, seeking to inflame popular passions. He took parliamentary attacks on his ministers personally, making criticism of their actions difficult by claiming full responsibility for whatever they had done. Despite the lofty elevation of his posture at Court, in politics he was too inclined to descend into the fray.

This was in part because Charles needed to be continually assured that his will was being properly obeyed. It made him careless of the elastic but enduring interdependence between redress of grievances and grants of supply, an integral part of the parliamentary process. For much the same reason, he was sparing in his explanations to Parliament. It was enough that he had declared his will. In his opening remarks to his first Parliament in 1625 and to the Short Parliament in 1640, he referred obliquely to his speech impediment; but his words, as reported, make it plain that he regarded the case for supply as beyond explanation or dispute. Yet Charles was also devious. His contortions in 1625 over the relaxation and enforcement of the penal laws at the time of his French marriage treaty and impending war with Spain did him no good in the eyes of many in Parliament. Fears were also quickly aroused that the balance of influence within the Church of England itself was being summarily shifted in an anti-Calvinist direction, making it harder for godly clergy to observe constraints on religious discussion which he had introduced in the interests of the peace of the Church. That Charles was reluctant to give ground gracefully was demonstrated by his ill-judged attempt to muffle the impact of the publication of the Petition of Right, a petty manoeuvre which further damaged his credibility. By 1629 he had shown in both England and Scotland that, whatever his doubts about his subjects, he did not himself inspire confidence.

In administration, Charles sometimes stood unusually close to business. Where James may well have deliberately limited his own attendances at the Privy Council's meetings in order to allow uninhibited discussion amongst his ministers, Charles was increasingly inclined to dominate its proceedings for extended periods with matters of direct concern to himself, especially financial ones. He was prepared to listen to arguments both at the Council table and, by preference, in the Bedchamber; but he usually took decisions alone and rarely explained his reasons. Buckingham apart, he had few close advisers; yet his government was in no sense isolated. Even before the duke's death, Court patronage drew as forthright a parliamentary critic as Wentworth into the fold, and others followed. Eliot himself hoped to do so. The presumption was still made, as it then had to be, that what was wrong with the King's administration was not Charles's own judgement but the nature and quality of the advice he received from his current ministers.

Yet Wentworth never felt wholly secure in the King's service. He held onto his presidency of the Council of the North after he was appointed Lord Deputy of Ireland, and his departure for Dublin in 1633 was preceded by extensive arrangements for safeguarding his interests on both sides of the Irish Sea, one aspect of which was his new closeness to Laud. The abrasiveness of his Irish administration owed as much to his desire to commend himself to the King, in the hope of returning to England, as it did to his naturally vigorous methods. Alone of Charles's dominions, Ireland felt the smack of 'Thorough'*; but the policies themselves were in essence traditional enough (**129**). Yet, although Wentworth made Ireland relatively prosperous and came close to bringing the country into line, he was continually unsure how he stood with the King. The forcefulness of his personality may indeed have dissuaded Charles from summoning him home to become Lord Treasurer on Portland's death in 1635. He would undoubtedly have invigorated the King's finances, but at what political cost? Wentworth's final return to England in 1640 allowed the release of internal tensions in Ireland which only his presence had held in check. As the political situation in Scotland continued to deteriorate, the close association between the Ulster settlers and the Scottish mainland was to become an important element in the breakdown of Charles's rule over his three kingdoms.

Scotland probably suffered most from the Stuarts' failure to develop a truly British aspect of their administration, and saw Charles at his worst. From his sweeping revocation onwards, he showed scant consideration for Scottish sensibilities or economic interests (**150**; Macinnes in **229**). His remodelling of the Privy Council and court of Sessions offended important lay interests, as did his appointment of bishops to offices of state. His summary treatment of Parliament in 1633, followed by the ill-founded trial of the dissident peer Balmerino for seditious libel in 1635, which was Scotland's counterpart to Hampden's case, all jarred badly. But the almost surreptitious introduction of a new liturgy, shortly after new canons, raised issues which transcended national boundaries.

The text of the liturgy was less Arminian than its provenance might have suggested; but at the time it seemed doubtful whether the Church was any longer in godly hands. The national covenant of 1637–38 bound the Calvinist clergy and laity in a common cause which held out the possibility of working for the deposition of ungodly princes wherever they might be found. By 1639 the covenanters were in arms, close to the border with England. This was heady stuff, far removed from mere peripheral discontents at central encroachment familiar in continental rebellions of this period. Instead, it aimed a challenge directly at the King's government, and, almost unavoidably, at Charles himself (**134**). In so far as there was a distinctively British problem, it was epitomised in the person of the King (**121**).

In England itself the challenge to ship money proceeded at the same time as the covenanting campaign. Both were seeking the recall of the English Parliament. How far convergence of interest brought cooperation in practice remains to be finally established; but evidence of a mutual sympathy and a shared awareness of current predicaments is not hard to find (**84**). In that sense Charles had, in his unhappy person, gone some way to uniting his disparate kingdoms. By 1640 he faced trouble on more fronts than he could readily handle, given the straitened nature of his finances (**182**). That limitation in no way inhibited him from taking the initiative, for, as always, he believed he was right. The Short Parliament, however, was more concerned with what had gone wrong in the recent past, and was in no hurry to grant sorely needed funds for use against the covenanters. In a session curtailed by early dissolution, John Pym's opening speech on 17 April for remedying the ills of the commonwealth took almost two hours to deliver. Subsequently, Charles's continued failure to settle with the Scots, and the entry on the King's side of the largely Catholic Irish army, raised the political stakes still further. The dissolution of Charles's three kingdoms into civil war was still some way off; but the mixture of strongly held convictions and deeply rooted mistrust was a volatile one.

# Part Five: Documents

(Note: spelling and punctuation have been modernised.)

**document 1**
## Prince Charles in Parliament, 1624

*Charles urges war primarily as a matter of honour; the religious dimension is missing.*

The King...intends you shall see that upon your counsel he was not able of himself and his own strength to engage himself in war without your assistance.... I desire you now to consider how the business is gone, that it requires expedition...how far the year is past; how far you have exasperated those who we conceive hereafter may be our enemies. Prepare yourselves so as that you may not show your teeth but bite also, if there be occasion.

Consider also how much the King's honour and mine much more is engaged if you should fail in this. It would be dishonourable to yourselves as well as to me. You shall oblige me who am now entering into the world and when time shall serve hereafter you shall not think your labours ill bestowed.

PRO, SP 14/160/65, Prince Charles to the Committee of Both Houses, 11 March 1624.

**document 2**
## The Prince's interest in revocation in the Principality, January 1625

*This is the first step in a major plan, confined to the principality of Scotland while Charles was still Prince, extended to the kingdom of Scotland after James's death in March 1625. Its origins are unclear, but James Stuart, Lord Ochiltree and Robert Johnston subsequently provided Charles with arguments justifying the change.*

I cannot think but your Lordship has heard of the course the Prince is on for the settling of his estate there, and how he is preparing for a revocation now before he be of full age [i.e., 25], and to this effect has written to the Chancellor [George Hay, Viscount Dupplin] and Secretary [Thomas Hamilton, Earl of Haddington] only, and that none of his Council more should be acquainted with it. The effect of his letter is that he may be satisfied in some questions that he has sent to them touching his own estate, specially touching the principality. His information comes from some there and, as I have heard, of the best quality.... I may assure you that the Prince his information is very punctual [i.e., precise] and particularly set down.

**24**, *Supplementary*, p. 218. Thomas Earl of Kellie at Whitehall to John Earl of Mar in Scotland, 24 January 1625.

### document 3
## Buckingham's relations with King Charles, 1625

*The Tuscan ambassador, Salvetti, here notes the successful completion of Buckingham's transition from old master to new, a difficult feat, rarely achieved.*

The Duke of Buckingham, although deeply grieved by the loss of the late King, his ever liberal master, may feel assured that the countenance and favour of the new King will be extended to him to a greater degree if it be possible. This is already shown by the most transparent evidence. He is with his Majesty all day; he sleeps in a room contiguous to the royal chamber; he has been confirmed in all his offices which are numerous and of the highest importance; and he has also been made Gentleman of the Bedchamber, and has received the golden key, the emblem of his office, so that he can, whenever he pleases, and at any hour, enter that chamber as well as any other part of the palace occupied by his Majesty. In fine, nothing is done without him.

**21**, p. 3.

### document 4
## The Commons at Oxford, August 1625

*A far cry from document 1. The £40,000 is the sum needed to get the fleet at Plymouth to sea. These MPs are all anxious to avoid a third successive grant of supply without any account being taken of parliamentary grievances.*

*(i) Edward Alford, 5 August:* That it was never the meaning of the House [in 1624] to be engaged; therefore all words which might receive any such interpretation were stricken out of the preamble of the [subsidy] act, and we ought now to be as careful [not] to grant subsidies in reversion.

*(ii) Sir Robert Phelips, 10 August:* If his Majesty's honour be in question, and he [be] in such necessity, they who have brought him to this strait have dishonoured the King, and if they have so ill disposed of the King and the state as that he cannot furnish so small a supply, they must bear the merits of their own counsel.... We are the last monarchy in Christendom that retain our original right and constitutions. Either his Majesty is able to set out this fleet, or it is not fit to go at all.

*(iii) Sir Francis Seymour, 10 August:* ...he was not satisfied touching the ground of this design, and has heard nothing to believe that it proceeded from good counsel. That which was taken into consideration by the Council of War and the Lords [of the Privy Council] was the proportion of money, men and munition, not how they should be employed.... It is unlikely he [i.e., Charles] should be in such great want as not to be able to disburse £40,000, and unfit for us, for such a sum, to deliver up the privileges of the House.

*(iv) Sir Thomas Wentworth, 10 August:* The word 'engagement' [is] a prejudicial word, as if we were less forward than the last Parliament. That they pretend the want of £40,000; he fears somewhat which may press us more in point of disadvantage than the sum. He is not against giving, but against this manner, to put us upon these straits to give or else to adjourn.

**36**, pp. 402, 448–9, 450, 451. See also **10**, p. 369, for drafts of Wentworth's speech.

## document 5
## Charles warns the burgh of Edinburgh, September 1625

*This extract illustrates Charles's uncertainty of tone. He expects absolute obedience, but feels the need to show its advantages. Note the similarity to the second paragraph of document 1.*

We persuade our selves you will be so much the more careful that in this beginning of our reign there be no matter of offence given us by you, whom we intend to benefit and favour in all business wherein you may happen hereafter to entreat us.

*Extracts from the Records of the Burgh of Edinburgh 1604–1626*, ed. M. Wood (Edinburgh, 1931), 276, Charles I to the Provost and other officers of Edinburgh, from Holbury, Hants, 1 September 1625.

## document 6
## Understanding Charles's meaning, October 1625

*Charles frequently refers to his lack of fluency; but he also found it convenient at times to be sparing in speech. His courtiers had to learn to interpret his meaning.*

His Majesty, as much with gesture as otherwise, gave me that am read in his dispositions (if I flatter not myself) apparent new confirmation of his especial good opinion of you, which I concluded and told him you were worthy of his favour and gracious opinion for many noble parts of knowledge and merit in you.

PRO, C115/N5/8632, Sir Roger Palmer, Master of the Household, to Sir John Scudamore, from the Court at Salisbury, 19 October 1625.

## document 7
## Charles finds extra work for Buckingham, October 1625

*The Duke has just seen the fleet off from Plymouth, and is preparing for his mission to Amsterdam and the Hague. Charles soon breaks into his rest. Dunkirk was in the Spanish Netherlands, and a rumour that its raiders intended to invade the Essex coast, as a pre-emptive strike, had been rife since late August. They had recently broken a Dutch blockade, and Warwick is very anxious for a gesture of support for his efforts in repairing rotting Elizabethan defences. James had nicknamed Buckingham 'Steenie' after the angelic-faced St Stephen; but he himself often spelt it as here. See also 38 and doc. 13.*

Stinie, here is advertisement that the Dunkirkers are come forth and lie all under the fort [at Dunkirk]. It hath given such an alarum to those countries [i.e. counties] lying over against it that, notwithstanding those orders which have been given, yet their fear so much overmasters their judgement that they neither know how to obey nor to resolve to defend themselves, but in disorder shamefully retire themselves. I know it is a cruelty to call you so soon from your wife, and I am sorry that my service doth enforce me to it at this time; yet such is the necessity of this occasion, that you must needs with all speed make your repair to Harwich where your stay will not be longer needful than for two or three days to give some countenance to my Lord Warwick's endeavours, since the Lord Lieutenant [i.e., the Earl of Sussex] hath in discontentment left the country [Essex]. Afterwards I give you leave to make your return to Kate [i.e., Buckingham's wife] without coming to me to give me an account, and then to stay till herself choose the time to send you to me.

BL, Harleian MSS 6988, f. 7r, Charles I to Buckingham, *c.* 14 October 1625.

**document 8**
# Charles and revocation in the kingdom of Scotland, January 1626

*John Erskine, Earl of Mar, the Scottish Treasurer, heads a delegation to Whitehall seeking clarification of the nature and extent of the new revocation. He finds Charles a very different proposition from his old schoolfellow, James VI and I. Charles's explanation in (iii) below illustrates the intensely personal way in which he regards the royal prerogative.*

*(i) 7 January*: Then Mar said unto his Majesty, that it was hard to [*sic*: for] any man to say unto him in particular any thing concerning that revocation, ·because for himself he had never seen it, but only once heard it read in the [Scottish Privy] Council, and he confessed he could not remember of every particular contained in it; but that in general it had put all his Majesty's subjects in great fear, for when that they thought it was intended that all their rights given by any of his Majesty's predecessors should be called in question, as also that it was not possible that his Majesty himself could make any right [i.e., grant] unto them but what might be called in question after his decease, they thought they were in a worse case than any subjects in the world.

**24** (1904), p. 135.

*(ii) 14 January*: And so Mar said, seeing your Majesty has time, for God['s] sake let not your laws want justice, for your Majesty can not imagine what grief it is to all your subjects; and seeing no time

can stay you to do what lawfully you may, for God's cause let them be douing [i.e., inactive] in the mean time that the subjects be not defrauded of justice, till you try what you may do lawfully. The King answered: My lord, it is better the subject suffer a little than all lie out of order. Sir, said Mar, you can not condemn them nor displace them until they be heard.

**24** (1904), p. 141.

*(iii) 9 February*: [Charles's explanation for his revocation was] because his Majesty, not coming to the crown in his minority, and so not having hurt the patrimony thereof himself, behoved for keeping of his royal prerogative to revoke what his predecessors had done to the hurt of the same.

*Register of the Privy Council of Scotland*, Second series, 1, 228.

**document 9**
# Laud on the need for peace in Church and state, February 1626

*This sermon at the opening of the 1626 Parliament, on the interdependence of harmony in Church and state, is a prelude to the proclamation of 14 June 1626 for the peace and quiet of the Church. Like the King, Laud is nervous of Calvinist links with 'popularity'.*

Would you keep the State in unity? In any case, take heed of breaking the peace of the Church. The peace of the State depends much upon it. For divide Christ in the minds of men, or divide the minds of men about their hope of salvation in Christ, and tell me what unity there will be. This so far as the Church is an ingredient into the unity of the State. But what other things are concurring to the unity of it, the State itself knows better than I can teach....

And one thing more I will be bold to speak out of a like duty to the Church of England, and the house of David. They, whoever they be, that would overthrow *sedes ecclesiae*, the seats of ecclesiastical government, will not spare, if ever they get power, to have a pluck at the throne of David. And there is not a man that is for parity, all fellows in the Church, but he is not for monarchy in the State. And certainly either he is but half-headed to his own principles, or he can be but half-hearted to the house of David.

**31**, vol. 1, pp. 71, 83.

# Dr Turner's Six Articles, 11 March 1626

*Turner's one moment of political prominence comes with these articles which, a trifle prematurely, launch the first full-scale attack on Buckingham. It is not clear how far he was prompted by his patron, Pembroke.*

1 Whether the Duke, being admiral, be not the cause of the loss of the King's royalty [i.e., regality] in the Narrow Seas?

2 Whether the unreasonable, exorbitant, and immense gifts of money and land bestowed on the Duke and his kindred, be not the cause of impairing the King's revenue, and impoverishing the Crown?

3 Whether the multiplicity of offices conferred upon the Duke, and others depending upon him (whereof they were not capable) be not the cause of the evil government of this kingdom?

4 Whether recusants in general, by a kind of connivancy, be not born out and increased, by reason of the Duke's mother and father-in-law [i.e., Earl of Rutland] being known papists?

5 Whether the sale of honours, offices and places of judicature, and ecclesiastical livings and promotions (a scandal and hurt to the kingdom) be not through the Duke?

6 Whether the Duke's staying at home, being admiral and general in the fleet of the sea and land army, were not the cause of the bad success and overthrow of that action [to Cadiz]; and whether he did give good direction for that design? (All these are famed to be so[i.e., grounded upon common fame].)

**40**, vol. 1, p. 217.

# The balance between supply and redress, March 1626

*Sir Ferdinando Fairfax, MP for Boroughbridge, shows his awareness of the delicate relationship between granting supply and having grievances redressed. Charles paid little heed to this.*

If we give nothing, we not only incense the King, who is in his own nature extremely stiff, but endanger a ruin of the Common-weal, as things now stand; and if we do give, it may perhaps not be employed the right way, and the more we part with, the more we shall want [i.e., lack] another time to bestow. If we give nothing we must expect to be dissolved, and live in apparent danger from abroad; if we give little, we must expect little from his Majesty in ease of our requests, and not be secure from our enemies. The proportion must make all things well or ill, and what this will be I yet know not, for Monday next [27 March] is the day appointed to begin this business, and without any intervening matter to proceed until we make an end.

**27**, vol. 1, p. 25. Sir Ferdinando Fairfax to his father, Sir Thomas Fairfax, at Denton, Yorkshire, 24 March 1626.

document 12

# A diarist notes reaction to the Forced Loan, April 1627

*This extract is from a fragmentary and anonymous diary, which provides some telling illustrations of the government's difficulties over the Forced Loan. It may be the work of the younger Harbottle Grimston, a Calvinist lawyer and MP, whose interests it amply reflects.*

*13 April* That if the Duke's peace can be made with some and a reconciliation with them then a parliament....

In London not one of forty yield to lend; that the Aldermen were at Court to show what little hope of the City. That the City were appointed to pay £20,000 to Burlamachi for the soldiers of the money they were to lend.

*14 April* The Attorney [General], asked if Essex men [i.e., the Chelmsford seven] came to the Star Chamber for refusing press money, said he thought not and said it had been well if that man had been dead that opened that gap.

That Sir Thomas Fanshawe should offer Essex men that if they would recant their refusal of press money, they should be at liberty; but would not.

Some courtiers and others daily at the Fleet [prison] to compliment with the gents that refuse.

*25 April* Sir John Wray, the President [of Council, Manchester]'s nephew refuseth; the President presseth him to lend, he will pay it for him. He [i.e., Wray] telleth him he doth him much dishonour to say that, for if he doth pay it for him, he will not repay it, neither will he visit him so oft[en] as he hath done.

PRO, SP 16/60/10, anonymous diary for 10–25 April 1627.

**document 13**
# A county stands up to the Council, April 1627

*This exchange illustrates the boldness, and desperation, of local governors like William Lord Maynard at this time, as well as their care to carry the county with them. Such men saved Charles from the consequences of some of his worst miscalculations during the war years, often as here without the help of experienced leaders removed from office by Buckingham after the 1626 Parliament, including Warwick. Essex had raised and spent £4,000 on manning – and mending – its defences, on a still unfulfilled promise of repayment by the Crown. Both in 1626 and 1627 Colchester, like most other ports, claimed inability to pay. The Council ordered the county to help; but when pressed hard, it was ready to accept the force of precedent. See also document 7.*

(i) We taking into consideration by what power we may tax the country for the setting forth of this ship [which Colchester had been asked for as a port] cannot find that there hath been any levy of this nature made by any other power but either by continued precedents or by the power derived unto us by a general and unanimous consent of the whole county. And not finding the warrant of any precedent of any taxation upon the county in this kind, we thought fit to have resort unto that other, of the consent of the country, from whom the payment of the money must come. And perceiving that neither his Majesty's service nor your lordships' directions would admit the necessary delay of our usual proceedings in the like cases, which hath been purposely to assemble the county together to receive their resolutions, we have taken the opportunity of these present sessions to communicate your lordships' letters with the grand jury\*, being the representative body of this county and drawn together from all parts thereof, who after some time of deliberation have returned unto us this answer which we are bold to send your lordships here enclosed.

**38**, no. 434. William Lord Maynard and other Deputy Lieutenants\* and Justices of the Peace of Essex to the Council from Quarter Sessions\*, 6 April 1627.

(ii) We have very seriously considered [whether the county should contribute to Colchester's ship money] . . . amongst our selves, and also with all the petty juries of this sessions and many other freeholders warned for the whole county, who did all with one consent desire to be excused. And our answer is [that] we are not able to perform the same in regard of the great expenses this county was at in Harwich camp and divers other charges since. And for as much as corporations have many privileges...it was never known that the whole shire did join with them in this kind.

**38**, no. 435. The Grand Jury's* answer, 5 April 1627.

(iii) ... We marvel very much at the course holden by you, and do not only condemn your indiscretions but have cause to suspect your affections in the managing of that service, holding it to be in effect the confronting of the counsel and directions of his Majesty and this Board with the counsel and discretions of a grand jury of Essex, as if they and you at a public sessions had a controlling power over the Acts of State; which carriage of yours deserves rather that you should be convented before the Board and sharply censured, than to be...admonished only by letter; upon which course we were resolved had not the remembrance of the good endeavours and affections shewed by some of you in former services mediated in your behalves.

**38**, no. 436. Privy Council to Essex JPs, 13 April 1627.

(iv) That upon receipt of the aforesaid letter [of 13 April] some of the Justices of Peace attended divers of the lords of the Council and made it appear unto them by shewing unto them the former book of precedents that they had proceeded in this business no otherwise in effect than had been done upon the like occasion in the year 1596. Whereupon their lordships were pleased to forebear any further proceedings therein.

**38**, no. 437. Memorandum, April 1627.

**document 14**

## The King presses the Loan, May 1627

*Charles's close identification with the Forced Loan makes refusal difficult. Ambitious gentry, at the head of recalcitrant counties, are uncertain which way to turn.*

My dear brother, I cannot hope to see you receive the least favour that the great ones can abridge you of, if you still refuse. Neither dare any move the King in the behalf of any gentleman refuser; for his heart is so inflamed in this business, as he vows a perpetual remembrance as well as a present punishment. And [al]though the

Duke will be gone shortly [bound for Rhé], yet no man can expect to receive any ease by his absence, since the King takes the punishment into his own direction.

**44**, vol. 1, p. 38. Henry Lord Clifford to his brother-in-law, Sir Thomas Wentworth, from St Martin's Lane, Strand, 20 May 1627.

**document 15**

## Buckingham's reported surprise at the recall of Parliament, February 1628

*The Duke had been playing political games over a possible recall; but there may well be some truth in this account.*

I was yester night at that office [Petty Bag in Chancery], where I found every man employed in making writs, which are to be ready for the seal on Tuesday next. My Lord Duke hath importuned the King for this parliament both publicly and privately ever since his return [from Rhé]. 'Tis thought his importunity was the greater in regard he was persuaded the King would never yield unto it; yet in his absence, upon others' motion, the King both yielded and signed the warrant and sent it away without acquainting the Duke therewith. That when it came to the Duke's knowledge, he would not believe it.

PRO, C115/N4/8579, Ralph Starkey to Sir John Scudamore, from London, 2 February 1628.

**document 16**

## The changing meaning of 'puritan', November 1628

*Davenant here gets to the heart of Calvinist disquiet at recent developments in the Church. He and Ward had been among the most moderate members of the Calvinist delegation James had sent to Dort in 1618, and yet were now to be branded puritan.*

Why that should now be esteemed puritan doctrine, which those [men] held who have done our Church the greatest service in beating down puritanism, or why men should be restrained from teaching that doctrine hereafter, which hitherto has been generally and publicly maintained, wiser men perhaps may, but I cannot, understand.

**98**, pp. 266–7. John Davenant, Bishop of Salisbury, to Dr Samuel Ward, Master of Sidney Sussex College, Cambridge, 4 November 1628.

**document 17**

## Charles's declaration at the end of Parliament, March 1629

*While not all criticism of his ministers in Parliament was principled, Charles as usual assumes here that none of it is. He is silent on the effects his handling of the Petition of Right may have had on a 'right understanding between us and our people'.*

Now all these things [i.e., religion, rights of the subject, national defences, maritime strength] that were the chief complaints the last session, being by our princely care so seriously reformed, the Parliament reassembled the 20th January last [1629]. We expected, according to the candour and sincerity of our own thoughts, that men would have framed themselves for the effecting of a right understanding between us and our people. But some few malevolent persons, like Empericks [i.e., charlatans or impostors] and lewd Artists, did strive to make new work, and to have some disease on foot, to keep themselves in request, and to be employed and entertained in the cure.... No sooner therefore was the Parliament set down but these ill-affected men began to sow and disperse their jealousies, by casting out some glances and doubtful speeches, as if the subject had not been so clearly and well dealt with, touching their liberties and touching the Petition [of Right] answered the last [session of] Parliament. This being a plausible theme, thought on for an ill purpose, easily took hold of the minds of many, that knew not the practice.

**40**, vol. 1, appendix, pp. 5–6.

**document 18**

## Calvinist despair, 1630

*This is an extract from a farewell sermon by the deprived minister-turned-lecturer Thomas Hooker, probably given on the first occasion he left England in 1630, after Laud's interest had, surprisingly slowly, been stirred. He had drawn large congregations to hear him preach at Chelmsford, where he had enjoyed Warwick's patronage and protection, after Colchester, which valued its independence, had refused to have him as town preacher. His manner in the pulpit seems to have been low-key and informative, and he was no 'fiery spirit'.*

For this is our misery, if that we have quietness and commodity we are well enough; thus we play mock-holy day with God. The gospel we make it our packhorse: God is going, his glory is departing, England hath seen her best days, and now evil days are befalling us: God is packing up his gospel because no body will buy his wares, nor come to his price.

Thomas Hooker, *The Danger of Desertion* (London, 1641), 15.

**document 19**

# Laud objects to finery in clerical dress, September 1631

*By temperament, and doubtless as a consequence of his Calvinist childhood, Laud had a strong preference for plainness in dress, a characteristic which gave him unexpected appeal in regions noted for their Calvinism, but which worried radicals like Henry Jessy, who feared a deeper point, and difference, was being missed. Winthrop had emigrated, partly for religious reasons, in 1629.*

[Laud at Kelvedon in north Essex] with much gravity and severity . . . . inveighed against the pride in the Ministry, that they must have their plush and satin and their silken cassocks, and their bandstrings with knots; if every knot had a bell at it, it would be a goodly show, saying if any would inform him of abuses in the ministry by drinking etc he would severely censure them. Mr Cook [one of the clergy] there, being commanded to attend him in his chamber, [had] got a black riband to his ruff, which he [Laud] so played upon: O what a show it would make if it were carnation or purple etc. He was very pleasant thus sometimes: by both which he drew the most people to admire him and applaud his proceedings.

*Winthrop Papers III 1631–1637* (Massachusetts Historical Society, 1943), 58. Henry Jessy to John Winthrop junior at Boston, New England, 9 January 1632.

**document 20**
# Oliver Cromwell on the death of Gustavus Adolphus, November 1632

*Cromwell was far from alone in following the fortunes of the Swedish King closely. English interest ran so high that, in October 1632, Charles, who had offered Gustavus little support, banned weekly gazettes of foreign news, because in reporting Swedish successes against the Habsburgs, they provided too sharp a contrast with his own recent efforts. Although Gustavus was killed shortly afterwards, Charles did not relax his ban until December 1638, apparently regarding the gazettes as prejudicial to his relations with Spain and as encouraging demands for a Parliament.*

He [Cromwell in June 1655] spoke much... of his late Majesty, King Gustav the Second and Great, of glorious memory, saying among other things that, being then a private person, he nevertheless had always followed his great campaigns with the greatest pleasure, had many times thanked God, with tears of joy in his eyes, for His gracious mercies, and when the tidings came of his death, had so mourned it that he could not scarcely believe that any Swede could mourn it more bitterly; for he saw that a great instrument to quell the power of the papists had been taken away.

*Swedish Diplomats at Cromwell's Court 1655–1656*, ed. Michael Roberts (Camden Society, 1988), 83–4.

**document 21**
# Neile's annual report for the province of York, 1633

*Neile may not have got much from Bishops Bridgeman and Potter, but he puts their case fairly, and may at the same time be pointing up the practical limitations to a system of reporting dreamed up by Laud and the King. Neile knew more about local administration than either.*

It may be your Majesty will ask how it cometh to pass that things should be suffered to be so generally out of order in those dioceses [i.e., Chester and Carlisle], the bishops being able and understanding men, professing all conformity in themselves and their care of requiring the like in others subject to their jurisdiction.

I must ingeniously confess I can neither justify nor excuse them. Yet this I know they will say, that finding their dioceses so distracted with papists and puritans, they thought by a mild way to recover the puritan part, least that, by carrying a severer hand upon the puritans than they had power to carry upon the papists, the popish party might take heart and opinion of favour. For the ordinary jurisdiction can proceed no further against popish recusants than to excommunicate, and certify those who do excommunicate themselves.

It may also be they will...say: it is in a manner impossible for the bishop to know how the public service is performed in every church and chapel of his diocese. The bishop can but enquire by the oaths of the churchwardens and sidesmen.

It may also be said in their excuse that the bishop executeth his jurisdiction by his inferior officers, his chancellor, his archdeacon, his commissaries and officers, and if they be negligent or corrupt it is not possible for the bishop to know and reform things that are amiss...be [he]...in his own person never so well disposed and affected to government.

PRO, SP 16/259/78, Neile to the King, January 1634.

document 22
## The shock of Prynne's punishment, May 1634

*D'Ewes, a godly lawyer and antiquary, had much fellow-feeling for Prynne; but he records another disquieting aspect of Charles's personal rule.*

He had been censured in the Star Chamber a few months before for some passages in a book he wrote against stage plays, called *Histrio-Mastix*, as if he had in them let slip some words tending to the Queen's dishonour, because he spoke of the unlawfulness of men's wearing women's apparel and women men's. Notwithstanding which, most men were affrighted to see that neither his academical nor barrister's gown could free him from the infamous loss of his ears.

*The Autobiography and Correspondence of Sir Simonds D'Ewes*, ed. J. O. Halliwell (2 vols, London, 1845) II, 104–5.

document 23
## Proceedings in the Forest of Dean, July 1634

*Rossingham, an experienced newsletter writer, reflects on the factional considerations which coloured the work of the Court of Justice Seat in Dean.*

My Lord Treasurer [Portland] is come back [from the Bath waters, where he had been for his health]. He makes no noise in the world, somewhat doth humble him, whether it be that his man Gibbons [his secretary] be found trespasser in the forest or that Sir John Winter, a papist, hath farmed the King's ironworks at £4,000 a year, and the woods of the same forest, or whether Sir John Finch his speech in his pleadings, which was that in '88 the Spanish design was (in case their invincible armado were overthrown) how they might destroy the forest of Dean, from whence our Navy was supplied, or that the chief destroyers of this forest at present were papists.

PRO, C115/M36/8427. Edmund Rossingham to John Viscount Scudamore, 1 August 1634.

**document 24**
# Charles's reluctance to touch for the King's Evil*, April 1636

*Peter Seddon's wife, Ellen, has come to London from Outwood, north of Manchester, some weeks previously in order to attend one of the supposedly regular ceremonies; but although her husband's old friend Walworth is steward to the Chamberlain of the Household, Pembroke, he can achieve nothing. Charles has to be reminded on this occasion that he must make his intentions plain, especially to those already in London from distant parts. He continued to touch in favoured cases.*

I have made forty journeys to Whitehall for Ellen but can do no good. The sickness begins in London and the King will suffer no diseased persons to come near him; yet there were some healed, but it was such as had some noble man's letter, and it was done privately in the garden. All the rest are sent away and appointed to come again at Michaelmas, if the sickness cease. You sent 6*d.* by her to drink, and I warrant you we have bought no land with it.

*The Correspondence of Nathan Walworth and Peter Seddon*, ed. J. S. Fletcher (Chetham Society, 1880), 41–2. Walworth from Baynard's Castle, London to Seddon, 21 April 1636.

**document 25**
# Whispering at Court for a Parliament, December 1636

*Lowe was a close associate of Cranfield and a lawyer with useful contacts at and around the Court. Like others, he reflects the serious loss of direction Charles's government suffered during the second half of 1636. Hence Charles's need to secure the legal foundations of annual, inland ship money.*

I have lately heard from a good hand that there is much private whispering at court of a Parliament and many great ones very affectionately bent that way, of whom the Lord Keeper [Coventry] and the Lord Treasurer [Juxon] (who they say affects not the present course and knows not how otherwise nor scarce with it to find means to discharge what is required of him) are two. I hear not the Lord Archbishop [Laud] named amongst the number. Those lords thus well affected to it have severally, as I hear, sent privately into several countries [i.e., counties] where they have most power to some of their intimate friends of quality to feel the disposition of the country whether it be likely they will now, seeing the King's ways, comply with his Majesty's ends, and have received some private answers back.

Kent Archives Office, U 269/1 CB 137. Anthony Lowe to Lionel Cranfield, Earl of Middlesex, 28 December 1636.

**document 26**
# The gentry of Kent on the judges' endorsement of ship money, February 1637

*These notes by Sir Roger Twysden, antiquarian and JP, provide an invaluable indication of gentry opinion about ship money after Baron Weston had addressed the assize court at Maidstone shortly after the judges' recent endorsement of the King's case for the levy.*

Some held ... that more could not be hoped for from a Prince than in causes of weight to proceed by the advice of his judges, and that [their] ... declaration ... was fully to the point, and by that the King had full right to impose it....

Others argued far differingly, that it could not but be expected that a just King would take counsel of his judges in a case of this weight, the greatest [that] was ever heard at a common [law] bar in England; that in a judgement that, not may but doth, touch every man in so high a point, every man ought to be heard and the reasons of every one weighed, which could not be but in Parliament... that the King hath no prerogative but that which the law of the land doth give and allow, and therefore his subjects could not with justice be denied a trial... that the Kings of this nation do in time of peace govern by their laws, in times of war by an absolute power; but the affirmation of a necessity could not be held to be one, for at home there was no likeli[hood] of any insurrection.

...There was much difference between the doing it by letter [i.e., raising ship money in the way Elizabeth and James had done], that being a kind of entreaty, and this way which was compulsory.

**90**, pp. 232–3.

## document 27
# The ship-money fleet's lack of purpose, July 1637

*While the judges and lawyers agonised over ship money, the fleet itself had very little to do.*

To ride in this place at anchor a whole summer together without hope of action, to see daily disorders in the fleet and not to have [the] means to remedy them, and to be in an employment where a man can neither do service to the state, gain honour to himself, nor do courtesies for his friends, is a condition that I think no body will be ambitious of.

**44**, vol. 2, p. 84. Earl of Northumberland to Wentworth, from the Downs, 15 July 1637.

## document 28
# Disorderliness at Court, December 1637

*Garrard shows how, by 1637, the effects of earlier reforms of the Household had worn off. He may have known that, very shortly, a sixteen-strong Council committee was to be set up, headed by Laud, Juxon, Coventry and Arundel, charged with identifying root problems since the reign of Henry VIII. It was, however, unable to reduce annual expenditure to its earlier levels.*

The Court is now filled with the families of every mean courtier.... The King's servants wait pell-mell without any order, lodge still in court, and feed there, though they be out of their month or quarter [i.e., the period of service]. Places are sold at strange rates all the court over, which makes men prey upon the King in the execution of the lowest places.

**44**, vol. 2, pp. 140–1. George Garrard to Wentworth, 16 December 1637.

**document 29**

## Laud's fears, June 1638

*No one else was as busy as Laud across a broad front during the 1630s, or so unremittingly attentive to administrative detail. Yet by 1638, he was taking a detached, and increasingly pessimistic, view of Charles's prospects. His experience as a Treasury commissioner 1635–36 had taught him much about the fragile state of the King's finances.*

It is not the Scottish business alone that I look upon, but the whole frame of things at home and abroad, with vast expenses out of little treasure, and my misgiving soul is deeply apprehensive of no small evils coming on. God in heaven avert them; but I can see no cure without a miracle, and I fear that will not be showed.

**31**, vol. 7, p. 456. Laud to Wentworth, 22 June 1638.

**document 30**

## The decision to end the Personal Rule, December 1639

*In October 1639 Charles had set up an eight-strong Council committee, headed by Wentworth (now called back to England) and Laud, with Hamilton as the only Scot, to advise on the Scottish problem in the wake of the First Bishops' War and the flimsy pacification at Berwick. Northumberland was also a member. They had several meetings with the Scottish treasurer, Traquair. Wentworth's views, reflected below, carried the day; but Charles took the precaution of gathering loans worth £200,000 from Privy Councillors before the year was out.*

This committee [of the Privy Council]...hath lately had several meetings to consider by what means the rebellious Scots should be brought to obedience.... The King's revenue, upon examination, appeared to be so anticipated, as little could be hoped for from thence; laying excises, enjoining each county to maintain a certain number of men whilst the war lasted and such like ways, were by some far pressed; but met with so many weighty objections that those lords that were all this while most averse to Parliaments, did now begin to advise the King's making trial of his people in Parliament, before he used any way of power. This being advised by their lordships (who to say truth, found themselves so puzzled that they knew not where to begin), the King was soon gained, and resolved the next Council day to propose it to the rest of the lords, which accordingly was done.... The day appointed for the meeting of Parliament is 13th of April next.

**8**, vol. 2, p. 623. Earl of Northumberland to Earl of Leicester, 12 December 1639.

# Glossary

*Book of Rates*   Contained the official valuations of commodities subject to customs duties. James I's book of 1604 was the first major revision since 1558; subsequent adjustments were more frequent, but official valuations generally lagged behind market values.

*Book of Sports*   Introduced by James I for Lancashire in 1617, and for the whole of England in 1618, to encourage recreation after divine worship on Sundays, much to the dismay of strict Calvinists. Reissued in 1633.

*Books of Orders*   Consisted of detailed sets of instructions from the Privy Council to the Justices of the Peace and their subordinate officials for coping with a pressing problem. The earliest book of all was issued to counter a visitation of plague in 1578, and was followed by one for reducing exceptionally high grain prices (or dearth) in January 1587. Others were issued as necessary thereafter: for plague in 1592, 1593, 1603, 1609, 1625, 1630, 1636 and 1646; for dearth in 1594, 1595, 1608, 1622 and 1630. The Book of Orders of 1631 was different, however: it was intended to be continuous, and to quicken the JPs' activities across a broader front. See **190, 169.**

*Civilians*   Lawyers trained in civil (or Roman) law, which they practised primarily in Church courts but also in those of the Admiralty.

*Customs farmers*   Syndicates of merchants and financiers who contracted with the Crown for the privilege of collecting customs duties. Their profits depended on the efficiency of their arrangements for collection.

*Deputy Lieutenants*   Small groups of senior gentry in each county who held their authority by deputation from their Lord Lieutenant(s), by whom they were by 1625 normally appointed. Earlier, James I had sometimes made the appointments himself.

Their responsibilities covered a wide range of military matters, including oversight of the trained bands*.

*Grand Jury* The senior jury of presentment at quarter sessions* and assizes, reporting regularly on administrative shortcomings, and from time to time offering comment – not always solicited by the bench – on current political anxieties; e.g., ship money in the 1630s. Generally regarded as the voice of the county. Each grand jury had seventeen or so members, of at least yeoman status.

*Justification by works* Justification is the change in man's condition by which, through God's grace, he passes from a state of sin to one of righteousness. Possible only by faith, according to the teachings of Luther and Calvin; but according to the Church of Rome, it might be attained by way of good works.

*King's Evil* Scrofula, which was supposedly curable by the king's touch. English monarchs customarily held touchings for the common people at regular and well-publicised intervals; but Charles I proved notably reluctant to do so. See **175**.

*Lecturers* Committed Calvinist clergy appointed by puritanical towns or godly patrons to fill relatively well-endowed preaching posts, providing an alternative or supplement to the parochial ministry. Their attitude to Church authority was often critical, and the more daring addressed political issues too. Bishops found such clergy difficult to control, and were disposed under Charles to suppress their lectureships.

*Militia* The domestic defence force, primarily the trained bands*.

*Patentees* Holders of letters patent under the Great Seal which authorised them to undertake the development or regulation of some form of commercial, industrial or administrative activity, with financial benefits to both the holders and the Crown; usually .....monopolistic . Important grants were considered beforehand by the Privy Council. Some patentees proved justifiably unpopular; but others behaved with the responsibility the Council hope for.

*Petty sessions* Local sessions of the Justices of the Peace, held in the interval between quarter sessions*. A customary practice from the middle of the 16th century in some counties but it had yet to acquire a settled form. Restricted to oversight of administrative matters.

*Predestination* A central tenet of Calvin's teaching, rejecting the universal saving will of God and maintaining that Christ's atoning death was offered for that minority of mankind, the Elect, who were the true believers. See **213**.

*Projectors* Often patentees*. An intending projector identified some aspect of administrative or commercial activity, which he might restore to its past efficiency or make effective for the first time, and, in return for royal approval, agreed to share his profits with the Crown. Widely disliked; but by no means all their undertakings were reprehensible: see, e.g., **201**.

*Quarter sessions* Formal sessions of the Justices of the Peace for disciplinary and administrative business, held in the counties in each season of the year. In their most usual, and probably most effective, form, convened as a single bench for the whole county; but a large minority of counties practised variants. Worked closely with assizes, a superior court held by two common law judges in almost all counties twice a year, and with petty sessions*.

*Supralapsarians* Those fundamentalist predestinarians who believed that, before the Fall, God had chosen a limited number of mankind for election to eternal salvation, while all the rest were condemned as reprobates. See **213**.

*The Lady Mora* The name by which Laud and Wentworth referred in their correspondence to the administration of Lord Treasurer Weston, which in their view was both incurably sluggish and deviously self-serving: the antithesis of 'Thorough'*. The Chancellor of the Exchequer, Cottington, was also guilty by association. Cast in feminine form, as was customary in their codes and cipher.

*Thorough* The term used by Laud and Wentworth to describe their favoured approach to public responsibilities. Broadly, it aimed at more efficient government and at more effective control by central authority of both Church and state; but its ends were never as well defined as its means. Not a practical proposition in England or Scotland; but applied by Wentworth in Ireland.

*Trained bands* Companies of horse and foot, raised and maintained by each county in readiness to defend it. The Privy Council expected the Deputy Lieutenants* to ensure regular mustering, adequate provision of arms and sufficient training. Bandsmen were generally in employment and were of more substance than the men pressed for service overseas, a liability from which the bands were exempt.

# Bibliography

Unless otherwise indicated, the place of publication is London.

Abbreviations used:

| | |
|---|---|
| *BIHR* | *Bulletin of the Institute of Historical Research* |
| CUP | Cambridge University Press |
| *Econ HR* | *Economic History Review* |
| *EHR* | *English Historical Review* |
| *HJ* | *Historical Journal* |
| *HLQ* | *Huntington Library Quarterly* |
| HMC | Historical Manuscripts Commission |
| *HR* | *Historical Research* (continuation of *BIHR*) |
| *HT* | *History Today* |
| *JBS* | *Journal of British Studies* |
| *JEH* | *Journal of Ecclesiastical History* |
| *NH* | *Northern History* |
| OUP | Oxford University Press |
| *PH* | *Parliamentary History* |
| *PP* | *Past and Present* |
| *THSLC* | *Transactions of the Historic Society of Lancashire and Cheshire* |
| *TRHS* | *Transactions of the Royal Historical Society* |

SOURCES

1 *Acts of the Privy Council of England*, ed. J. R. Dasent *et al.*, 46 vols, 1542–1631, HMSO, 1890–1964. Thereafter published on micro-opaque fiche to 31 May 1637, and then in facsimile to 30 August 1645.

2 Ashton, R., *James I by his Contemporaries*, Hutchinson, 1975.

3 Baillie, R., *The Letters and Journals*, ed. D. Laing, 3 vols, Bannatyne Club, Edinburgh, 1841–42.

4 *Calendar of State Papers, Domestic*, Edward VI to James I, ed. R. Lemon *et al.*, 12 vols, 1856–72.

5 *Calendar of State Papers, Domestic*, Charles I, ed. J. Bruce *et al.*, 23 vols, 1858–97.

**6** *Calendar of State Papers, Venetian*, ed. A. B. Hinds, vols 10–25, 1900–25.

**7** Clarendon, Edward Hyde, first Earl of, *History of the Rebellion*, ed. W. D. Macray, 6 vols, OUP, 1888.

**8** Collins, A. (ed.), *Letters and Memorials of State*, 2 vols, 1746.

**9** *The Commons Debates for 1629*, ed. W. Notestein and F. H. Relf, Minnesota University Press, 1921.

**10** Cooper, J. P. (ed.), *The Wentworth Papers 1597–1628*, Camden Society, 1973.

**11** Corbett, J. S. (ed.), *Fighting Instructions 1530–1816*, Navy Records Society, 1905.

**12** Cosin, J., *The Correspondence of John Cosin D. D.*, ed. G. Ornsby, 2 vols, Surtees Society, 1868, 1872.

**13** D'Ewes, S., *The Diary of Sir Simonds D'Ewes 1622–1624*, ed. E. Bourcier, Didier, Paris, 1974.

**14** Donaldson, G. (ed.), *Scottish Historical Documents*, Scottish Academic Press, 1974.

**15** Finet, J., *Ceremonies of Charles I. The Notebooks of John Finet 1628–1641*, ed. A. J. Loomie, Fordham University Press, 1987.

**16** Gardiner, S. R. (ed.), *The Constitutional Documents of the Puritan Revolution 1625–1660*, OUP, 3rd edn revised, 1951.

**17** Grosart, A. B. (ed.), *The Voyage to Cadiz in 1625*, Camden Society, 1883.

**18** Hacket, J., *Scrinia Reserata*, 2 vols, 1692.

**19** HMC 2, *Third Report*, appx, 1872.

**20** HMC 8, *Ninth Report*, appx 2, 1883.

**21** HMC 16, *Skrine (Salvetti) MSS*, 1883.

**22** HMC 33, *MSS of the Earl of Lonsdale*, 1893.

**23** HMC 45, *Buccleuch (Montagu House) MSS*, vols 1 and 3, 1899, 1926.

**24** HMC 60, *Mar and Kellie MSS 1356–1743*, 1904, and *Supplementary*, 1930.

**25** Holles, J., *The Letters of John Holles 1587–1637*, ed. P. R. Seddon, 3 vols, Thoroton Society, 1975–86.

**26** James I, *The Political Works of James I*, ed. C. H. McIlwain, Harvard University Press, 1918.

**27** Johnson, G. W. (ed.), *The Fairfax Correspondence: Memoirs of the Reign of Charles the First*, 2 vols, Richard Bentley, 1848.

**28** Kenyon, J. P. (ed.), *The Stuart Constitution*, CUP, 2nd edn, 1986.

29   Larkin, J. F. and Hughes, P. L. (eds), *Stuart Royal Proclamations, I: 1603–1625*, OUP, 1973.

30   Larkin, J. F. (ed.), *Stuart Royal Proclamations, II: 1625–1646*, OUP, 1983.

31   Laud, W. *The Works of William Laud, D. D.*, ed. W. Scott and J. Bliss, 7 vols, Oxford, 1847–60.

32   McGowan, A. P. (ed.), *The Jacobean Commissions of Enquiry 1608 and 1618*, Navy Records Society, 1971.

33   Nichols, J., *The Progresses ... of King James the First*, 4 vols, 1828.

34   Pett, P., *The Autobiography of Phineas Pett*, ed. W. G. Perrin, Navy Records Society, 1918.

35   Phillips, C. B. (ed.), *Lowther Family Estate Books 1617–1675*, Surtees Society, 1979.

36   *Proceedings in Parliament 1625*, ed. M. Jansson and W. B. Bidwell, Yale University Press, 1987.

37   *Proceedings in Parliament 1628*, ed. M. F. Keeler *et al.*, 6 vols, Yale University Press, 1977–83.

38   Quintrell, B. W. (ed.), *The Maynard Lieutenancy Book 1608–1639*, Essex Historical Documents, Essex Record Office, 2 vols, 1993.

39   Rubens, P. P., *The Letters of Peter Paul Rubens*, ed. R. S. Magurn, Harvard University Press, 1955.

40   Rushworth, J., *Historical Collections*, 7 vols, 1659–1701.

41   Searle, A. (ed.), *Barrington Family Letters 1628–1632*, Camden Society, 1983.

42   Schofield, B. (ed.), *The Knyvett Letters 1620–1644*, Constable, 1949.

43   Spedding, J. (ed.), *The Letters and Life of Francis Bacon*, 7 vols, Longman, 1862–74.

44   Strafford, Thomas Wentworth, Earl of, *Strafford's Letters and Despatches*, ed. W. Knowler, 2 vols, 1739.

SECONDARY WORKS

45   Adams, S., 'The road to La Rochelle: English foreign policy and the Huguenots, 1610–1629', *Proceedings of the Huguenot Society of London*, 22 (1975).

46   Anderson, M. S., *War and Society in Europe of the Old Regime*, Fontana, 1989.

47   Andrews, K. R., *Ships, Money and Politics*, CUP, 1991.

48   Ashton, R., 'Conflicts of concessionary interest in early

Stuart England', in D.C. Coleman and A.H. John (eds), *Trade, Government and Economy in pre-Industrial England*, Weidenfeld & Nicolson, 1976.

**49** Ashton, R., *The City and the Court 1603–1643*, CUP, 1979.

**50** Ashton, R., *The Crown and the Money Market 1603–1640*, OUP, 1960.

**51** Ashton, R., 'The disbursing official under the early Stuarts: the cases of Sir William Russell and Philip Burlamachi', *BIHR* 30 (1957).

**52** Aston, M., *England's Iconoclasts*, vol. I, OUP, 1989.

**53** Aylmer, G.E., 'Attempts at administrative reform 1625–1640', *EHR* 72 (1957).

**54** Aylmer, G.E., 'Buckingham as an administrative reformer?', *EHR* 105 (1990).

**55** Aylmer, G.E., *The King's Servants. The Civil Service of Charles I 1625–1642*, Routledge & Kegan Paul, 1961.

**56** Aylmer, G.E., *The Personal Rule of Charles I 1629–1640*, Historical Association, New Appraisals in History, 14, 1989.

**57** Bard, N.P., 'The ship money case and William Fiennes, Viscount Saye and Sele', *BIHR* 50 (1977).

**58** Barnes, T.G., *Somerset 1625–1640*, OUP, 1961.

**59** Barnes, T.G., 'County politics and a puritan *cause célèbre:* Somerset churchales 1633', *TRHS*, 1959.

**60** Bernard, G.W., 'The Church of England *c.* 1529–1642', *History* 75 (1990).

**61** Bowle, J., *Charles the First*, Weidenfeld & Nicolson, 1975.

**62** Boynton, L., 'Billeting: the example of the Isle of Wight', *EHR* 74 (1959).

**63** Boynton, L., 'Martial Law and the Petition of Right', *EHR* 79 (1964).

**64** Boynton, L., *The Elizabethan Militia*, Routledge & Kegan Paul, 1967.

**65** Butler, M., 'Early Stuart court culture: compliment or criticism?', *HJ* 32 (1989) (review article).

**66** Butler, M., *Theatre and Crisis 1632–1642*, CUP, 1984.

**67** Carlton, C., *Archbishop William Laud*, Routledge & Kegan Paul, 1987.

**68** Carlton, C., *Charles I: the Personal Monarch*, Routledge & Kegan Paul, 1983.

**69** Cogswell, T., 'A low road to extinction? Supply and redress of grievances in the parliaments of the 1620s', *HJ* 33 (1990).

**70** Cogswell, T., *The Blessed Revolution*, CUP, 1989.

71   Cogswell, T., 'Foreign policy and parliament: the case of La Rochelle, 1625–1628', *EHR* 99 (1984).

72   Cooper, J. P., 'The fall of the Stuart monarchy', in *The New Cambridge Modern History IV: the Decline of Spain and the Thirty Years' War*, ed. J. P. Cooper, CUP, 1970.

73   Cope, E., *Politics without Parliaments 1629–1640*, Allen & Unwin, 1987.

74   Coward, B., *The Stuart Age 1603–1714*, Longman, 1980.

75   Cressy, D., *Bonfires and Bells*, Weidenfeld & Nicolson, 1989.

76   Croft, P., 'Fresh light on Bate's case', *HJ* 30 (1987).

77   Cuddy, N., 'The revival of the entourage: the Bedchamber of James I 1603–1625', in D. Starkey *et al.*, *The English Court*, Longman, 1987.

78   Cust, R., *The Forced Loan and English Politics 1626–1628*, OUP, 1987.

79   Cust, R., 'Charles I and a draft declaration for the 1628 parliament', *HR* 63 (1990).

80   Cust, R., 'Charles I, the Privy Council and the forced loan', *JBS* 24 (1985).

81   Cust, R., 'News and politics in early seventeenth-century England', *PP* 112 (1986).

82   Cust, R. and Hughes, A. (eds), *Conflict in Early Stuart England*, Longman, 1989.

83   Dalton, C., *The Life and Times of General Sir Edward Cecil, Viscount Wimbledon*, 2 vols, Sampson Low, 1885.

84   Donald, P., *An Uncounselled King*, CUP, 1990.

85   Duffy, E., 'The godly and the multitude in Stuart England', *The Seventeenth Century*, 1 (1986).

86   Dures, A., *English Catholicism 1558–1642*, Longman, 1983.

87   Ehrman, J. R., *The Navy in the Wars of William III 1689–1697*, CUP, 1953.

88   Elton, G. R., 'A high road to civil war?' in C. H. Carter (ed.), *From the Renaissance to the Counter-Reformation*, Cape, 1966.

89   Fielding, J., 'Opposition to the personal rule of Charles I: the diary of Robert Woodford 1637–1641', *HJ* 31 (1988).

90   Fincham, K., 'The judges' decision on ship money in February 1637: the reaction of Kent', *BIHR* 57 (1984).

91   Fincham, K., 'Prelacy and politics: archbishop Abbot's defence of protestant orthodoxy', *HR* 61 (1988).

92   Fincham K. and Lake, P., 'The ecclesiastical policy of James I', *JBS* 24 (1985).

93   Flemion, J. S., 'The dissolution of parliament in 1626: a

revaluation', *EHR* 87 (1972).

**94** Fletcher, A., *A County Community in Peace and War: Sussex 1600–1660*, Longman, 1975.

**95** Fletcher, A., *Reform in the Provinces*, Yale University Press, 1986.

**96** Foster, A. 'The function of a bishop: the case of Richard Neile 1562–1640', in R. O'Day and F. Heal (eds), *Continuity and Change*, Leicester University Press, 1976.

**97** Foster, E. R., 'Printing the Petition of Right', *HLQ* 38 (1974–75).

**98** Fuller, M., *The Life, Letters and Writings of John Davenant*, Methuen, 1897.

**99** Gardiner, S. R., *The History of England 1603–1642*, 10 vols, Longman, 1893 edn.

**100** Gordon, M. D., 'The collection of ship money in the reign of Charles I', *TRHS*, 1910.

**101** Gregg, P., *King Charles I*, Dent, 1981.

**102** Guy, J. A., 'The origins of the Petition of Right reconsidered', *HJ* 25 (1982).

**103** Hammersley, G., 'The revival of the forest laws under Charles I', *History* 45 (1960).

**104** Harrison, G. A., 'Innovation and precedent: a procedural reappraisal of the 1625 parliament', *EHR* 102 (1987).

**105** Havran, M. J., *Caroline Courtier: the Life of Lord Cottington*, Macmillan, 1973.

**106** Havran, M. J., 'The character and principles of an English king: the case of Charles I', *The Catholic Historical Review* 69 (1983).

**107** Heal, F., 'The archbishop of Canterbury and the practice of hospitality', *JEH* 33 (1982).

**108** Heal, F., 'Archbishop Laud revisited: leases and estate management at Canterbury and Winchester before the Civil War', in R. O'Day and F. Heal (eds), *Princes and Paupers*, Leicester University Press, 1981.

**109** Hibbard, C., *Charles I and the Popish Plot*, University of North Carolina Press, 1983.

**110** Hill, C., *Antichrist in Seventeenth-century England*, OUP, 1971.

**111** Hill, C., *The Economic Problems of the Church*, OUP, 1956.

**112** Hirst, D., *Authority and Conflict in England 1603–1658*, Arnold, 1986.

**113** Hirst, D., 'Parliament, law and war in the 1620s', *HJ* 23 (1980) (review article).

114  Hirst, D., 'The Privy Council and the problems of enforcement in the 1620s', *JBS* 18 (1978).
115  Hirst, D., *The Representative of the People?*, CUP, 1975.
116  Hirst, D., 'Revisionism revised: the place of principle', *PP* 92 (1981).
117  Holmes, C., *Seventeenth-century Lincolnshire*, History of Lincolnshire Committee, 1980.
118  Holmes, C., 'The county community in Stuart historiography', *JBS* 19 (1980).
119  Hoyle, D., 'The Commons investigation of Arminianism and popery in Cambridge on the eve of the Civil War', *HJ* 29 (1986).
120  Hughes, A., *Politics, Society and Civil War in Warwickshire 1620–1660*, CUP, 1987.
121  Hughes, A., *The Causes of the English Civil War*, Macmillan, 1991.
122  Hughes, A., 'Thomas Dugard and his circle in the 1630s – a "parliamentary-puritan" problem', *HJ* 29 (1986).
123  Hunt, W., *The Puritan Moment: the Coming of Revolution in an English County*, Harvard University Press, 1983.
124  Hunt, W., 'Spectral origins of the English revolution: legitimate courses in early Stuart England', in G. Eley and W. Hunt (eds), *Reviving the English Revolution*, Verso, 1988.
125  Israel, J. I., *The Dutch Republic and the Hispanic World 1606–1661*, OUP, 1982.
126  Jones, W. J., *Politics and the Bench*, Allen & Unwin, 1971.
127  Jones, W. J., 'The "Great Gamaliell of the Law", Mr Attorney Noye', *HLQ* 40 (1977).
128  Judges, A. V., 'Philip Burlamachi: a financier of the Thirty Years' War', *Economica* 6 (1926).
129  Kearney, H. F., *Strafford in Ireland: a Study in Absolutism*, 2nd edn, CUP, 1980.
130  Kearney, H., 'Strafford in Ireland, 1633–1640', *HT* 39 (1989).
131  Kepler, J. S., 'Fiscal aspects of the English carrying trade during the Thirty Years' War', *Econ HR*, 1972.
132  Kepler, J. S., *The Exchange of Christendom*, Leicester University Press, 1976.
133  King, P., 'Bishop Wren and the suppression of the Norwich lecturers', *HJ* 11 (1968).
134  Koenigsberger, H., '*Dominium Regale* or *Dominium Politicum et Regale*: monarchies and parliaments in early modern

Europe', in H. G. Koenigsberger (ed.), *Politicians and Virtuosi*, The Hambledon Press, 1986.

**135** Kopperman, P. E., *Sir Robert Heath 1574–1649*, Royal Historical Society, 1989.

**136** Lake, P., 'Anti–popery: the structure of a prejudice', in **82**.

**137** Lake, P., 'Calvinism and the English Church 1570–1635', *PP* 114 (1987).

**138** Lake, P., 'The collection of ship money in Cheshire during the sixteen-thirties: a case study in relations between central and local government', *NH* 17 (1981).

**139** Lambert, S., 'Committees, religion and parliamentary encroachment on royal authority in early Stuart England', *EHR* 105 (1990).

**140** Lambert, S., 'Procedure in the House of Commons in the early Stuart period', *EHR* 95 (1980).

**141** Lambert, S., 'Richard Montagu, arminianism and censorship', *PP* 124 (1989).

**142** Lamont, W., *Godly Rule*, Macmillan, 1969.

**143** Lamont, W., *Marginal Prynne*, Routledge & Kegan Paul, 1963.

**144** Leonard, H. H., 'Distraint of knighthood: the last phase 1625–1641', *History* 63 (1978).

**145** Lockyer, R., *Buckingham*, Longman, 1981.

**146** Lockyer, R., *The Early Stuarts*, Longman, 1989.

**147** Lockyer, R., 'An English *valido*? Buckingham and James I', in R. Ollard and P. Tudor-Craig (eds), *For Veronica Wedgwood These: Studies in Seventeenth-century History*, Collins, 1986.

**148** Loomie, A. J., 'The Spanish faction at the court of Charles I', *BIHR* 59 (1986).

**149** Macalpine, I. *et al.*, 'Porphyria in the royal houses of Stuart, Hanover and Prussia', *British Medical Journal* 6 (1968).

**150** Macinnes, A. I., *Charles I and the Making of the Covenanting Movement 1625–1641*, John Donald, 1991.

**151** Marchant, R. A., *The Church under the Law*, CUP, 1969.

**152** Marchant, R. A., *Puritans and the Church Courts in the Diocese of York*, Longman, 1960.

**153** Millar, O., *The Age of Charles I*, The Tate Gallery, 1972.

**154** Millar, O., *Van Dyck in England*, National Portrait Gallery, 1982.

**155** Moody, T. W., Martin, F. X., and Byrne, F. J. (eds), *Early Modern Ireland 1534–1691*, OUP, 1976.

156 Morrill, J., 'Sir William Brereton and England's wars of religion', *JBS* 24 (1985).

157 Morrill, J., 'The religious context of the English Civil War', *TRHS*, 1984.

158 Morrill, J., *The Revolt of the Provinces*, 2nd edn, Longman, 1980.

159 Oppenheim, M., *A History of the Administration of the Royal Navy*, new edn, with introduction by K. R. Andrews, Temple Smith, 1988.

160 Parker, G., *The Thirty Years' War*, Routledge & Kegan Paul, 1984.

161 Pearl, V., *London and the Outbreak of the Puritan Revolution*, OUP, 1961.

162 Pennington, D. H., *Seventeenth-century Europe*, Longman, 1970.

163 Pettit, P. A. J., *The Royal Forests of Northampton 1558–1714*, Northamptonshire Record Society, 1968.

164 Popofsky, L. S., 'The crisis over tonnage and poundage in parliament in 1629', *PP* 126 (1990).

165 Prest, W., 'Ship money and Mr Justice Hutton', *HT* 41 (1991).

166 Quinn, D. B. and Ryan, A. N., *England's Sea-Empire*, Allen & Unwin, 1983.

167 Quintrell, B. W., 'Charles I and his navy in the 1630s', *The Seventeenth Century* 3 (1988).

168 Quintrell, B. W., 'Lancashire ills, the king's will and the troubling of Bishop Bridgeman', in C. B. Phillips and J. I. Kermode (eds), *Seventeenth-century Lancashire, THSLC* 132 (1983); also *THSLC* 137 (1988).

169 Quintrell, B. W., 'The making of Charles I's Book of Orders', *EHR* 95 (1980).

170 Ralph, P. L., *Sir Humphrey Mildmay, Royalist Gentleman*, Rutgers University Press, 1947.

171 Ranum, O. A., *Richelieu and the Councillors of Louis XIII*, OUP, 1963.

172 Reeve, L. J., *Charles I and the Road to Personal Rule*, CUP, 1989.

173 Reeve, L. J., 'Sir Robert Heath's advice for Charles I in 1629', *BIHR* 59 (1986).

174 Reeve, L. J., 'The arguments in King's Bench in 1629 concerning the imprisonment of John Selden and other Members of the House of Commons', *JBS* 25 (1986).

175 Richards, J., '"His Nowe Majestie" and the English

monarchy: the kingship of Charles I before 1640', *PP* 113 (1986).

**176** Roberts, M., *Gustavus Adolphus: a History of Sweden 1611–1632*, 2 vols, Longman, 1953, 1958.

**177** Robertson, J. C., 'Caroline culture: bridging court and country', *History* 75 (1990).

**178** Russell, C., *Parliaments and English Politics 1621–1629*, OUP, 1979.

**179** Russell, C., 'Parliamentary history in perspective 1604–1629', *History* 61 (1976).

**180** Russell, C., 'The ship money judgements of Bramston and Davenport', *EHR* 77 (1962).

**181** Russell, C., *The Causes of the English Civil War*, OUP, 1990.

**182** Russell, C., *The Fall of the British Monarchies 1637–1642*, OUP, 1991.

**183** Seaver, P., *The Puritan Lectureships*, Stanford University Press, 1970.

**184** Sharp, B., *In Contempt of All Authority*, California University Press, 1980.

**185** Sharpe, K., 'Archbishop Laud', *HT* 33 (1983).

**186** Sharpe, K., *Criticism and Compliment: the Politics of Literature in the England of Charles I*, CUP, 1987.

**187** Sharpe, K., 'Faction at the early Stuart court', *HT* 33 (1983).

**188** Sharpe, K., *Politics and Ideas in Early Stuart England*, Pinter Publishers, 1989.

**189** Sharpe, K. (ed.) *Faction and Parliament*, OUP, 1978.

**190** Slack, P., 'Books of Orders: the making of English social policy 1577–1631', *TRHS* 1980.

**191** Smith, A. H., 'Militia rates and militia statutes 1558–1663', in P. Clark *et al.* (eds), *The English Commonwealth 1547–1640*, Leicester University Press, 1979.

**192** Smuts, R. M., *Court Culture and the Origins of a Royalist Tradition in Stuart England*, University of Pennsylvania Press, 1987.

**193** Smuts, R. M., 'The puritan followers of Henrietta Maria in the 1630s', *EHR* 93 (1978).

**194** Snow V., 'The Arundel case, 1626', *The Historian* 26 (1964).

**195** Sommerville, J. P., *Politics and Ideology in England 1603–1640*, Longman, 1986.

**196** Springell, F. C., *Connoisseur and Diplomat*, Maggs Bros Ltd, 1963.

197 Stearns, S.J., 'Conscription and English society in the 1620s', *JBS* 11 (1972).

198 Strong, R., *Henry Prince of Wales and England's Lost Renaissance*, Thames & Hudson, 1986.

199 Swales, R.J.W., 'The ship money levy of 1628', *BIHR* 50 (1977).

200 Taylor, H. 'Trade, neutrality and the "English Road", 1630–1648', *Econ HR*, 1972.

201 Thirsk, J., 'Projects for gentlemen, jobs for the poor: mutual aid in the Vale of Tewkesbury 1600–1630', in P. McGrath and J. Cannon (eds), *Essays in Bristol and Gloucestershire History*, Bristol and Gloucester Archaeological Society, 1976.

202 Thomas, P.W., 'Charles I of England: the tragedy of absolutism', in A.G. Dickens (ed.), *The Courts of Europe*, Thames & Hudson, 1977.

203 Thompson, C., 'Court politics and parliamentary conflict in 1625', in **82.**

204 Thompson, C., *Parliamentary History in the 1620s: In or Out of Perspective?*, The Orchard Press, Wivenhoe, 1986.

205 Thompson, C., 'The divided leadership of the House of Commons in 1629', in **189.**

206 Thompson, C., 'The origins of the politics of the parliamentary Middle Group, 1625–1629', *TRHS*, 1972.

207 Thrush, A., 'In pursuit of the frigate 1603–1640', *HR* 64 (1991).

208 Tillbrook, M.J., 'Arminianism and society in County Durham 1617–42', in D. Marcombe (ed.), *The Last Principality: Politics, Religion and Society in the Bishopric of Durham 1494–1660*, University of Nottingham, 1987.

209 Tite, C.G.C., *Impeachment and Parliamentary Judicature in Early Stuart England*, Athlone Press, 1974.

210 Tomlinson, H. (ed.), *Before the English Civil War*, Macmillan, 1983.

211 Trevor-Roper, H.R., *Catholics, Anglicans and Puritans*, Secker & Warburg, 1987.

212 Trevor-Roper, H.R., *Archbishop Laud*, Macmillan, 2nd edn, 1962.

213 Tyacke, N., *Anti-Calvinists: the Rise of English Arminianism c. 1590–1640*, OUP, 1987.

214 Tyacke, N., 'Arminianism and English culture', in A.C. Duke and C.A. Tamse (eds), *Britain and the Netherlands*, Martinus Nijhoff, 1982.

## Bibliography

**215** Tyacke, N., 'Puritanism and Counter-Revolution', in C. Russell (ed.), *The Origins of the English Civil War*, Macmillan, 1973.

**216** Tyacke, N., 'Science and religion at Oxford before the Civil War', in D. H. Pennington and K. Thomas (eds), *Puritans and Revolutionaries*, OUP, 1978.

**217** White, P., 'The rise of Arminianism reconsidered', *PP* 101 (1983).

**218** Wilkinson, D. J. 'The commission of peace in Lancashire, 1603–1642', in C. B. Phillips and J. I. Kermode (eds), *Seventeenth-century Lancashire, THSLC* 132 (1983).

**219** Wormald, J., 'James VI and I: two kings or one?', *History* 68 (1983).

**220** Young, M. B., 'Buckingham, war and parliament: revisionism gone too far', *PH* 4 (1985).

**221** Young, M. B., 'Revisionism and the Council of War, 1624–1626', *PH* 8 (1989).

**222** Young, M. B., *Servility and Service: the Life and Work of Sir John Coke*, Royal Historical Society, 1986.

**223** Zagorin, P., 'Sir Edward Stanhope's advice to Thomas Wentworth, viscount Wentworth, concerning the deputyship of Ireland: an important letter of 1631', *HJ* 7 (1964).

**224** Zaller, R., 'The concept of opposition in early Stuart England', *Albion* 12 (1980).

ADDENDA

**225** Fissel, M. C. (ed.), *War and Government in Britain 1598–1650*, Manchester University Press, 1991.

**226** HMC 77, *De L'Isle and Dudley MSS*, vol. 6, 1966.

**227** *The Camden Miscellany*, vol. 6, 1871; (b) 'The Earl of Bristol's Defence', ed. S. R. Gardiner.

**228** *The Proceedings in Parliament ... 4 April 1628* (1628).

**229** Wormald, J. (ed.), *Scotland Revisited*, Collins & Brown, 1991.

**230** Cogswell T., 'The politics of propaganda.. in the 1620s', *JBS* 2 9 (1990).

**231** Cust R., 'Charles I and the parliament of 1628', *TRHS* 1992.

**232** Cust R., 'Anti- puritanism and urban politics', *HJ* 25 (1992).

**233** Sharpe K., *The Personal Rule of Charles I*, Yale UP, 1992.

# Index